Understand Investment Clubs in a Day

Neil Poyner
Calum Campbell

TTL is an imprint of
Take That Ltd.
P.O.Box 200,
Harrogate
HG1 2YR
ENGLAND

email:sales@takethat.co.uk

www.takethat.co.uk

10 9 8 7 6 5 4 3 2 1

You should take independent financial advice before acting on material contained in this book.

TTL are always keen to receive ideas and manuscripts for new financial books. Please send details to the address above.

ISBN 1-873668-96-1

Contents

Acknowledgements

Thanks to Eamonn for initial inspiration and later guidance, understanding wives for allowing us to burn the midnight oil when required, Martin for supplying his graphics skills, and the now-expired Loss Amigo's Investment Club for invaluable experiences.

Neil Poyner
Calum Campbell

In the same series...
Understand Shares in a Day
Understand Bonds & Gilts in a Day
Understand Day Trading in a Day
Understand Derivatives in a Day
Understand Financial Risk in a Day
Understand Commodities in a Day
Understand Swaps in a Day

Introduction

UNDERSTAND INVESTMENT CLUBS IN A DAY provides concise and relevant information that you can use easily and effectively. It identifies and explains all aspects of an Investment Club; how to join one, how to set up a club, the pitfalls that you should be aware of and the necessities for survival and longevity.

The authors have over ten years of directly related experience as club members and elected officers in both highly successful and less successful Investment Clubs - so they can provide insight into the benefits and also problems that may arise. They currently hold shares in a thriving Investment Club and also maintain personal share portfolios.

An Investment Club is a group of people who are prepared to pool resources and invest as a collective, usually in stocks and shares. The club can be formed from colleagues at a workplace, by families or simply by a group of friends who share a common interest in finance.

People from all walks of life, a variety of backgrounds and financial prowess join Investment Clubs. You do not need to be wealthy and there are no restrictions or limitations. You will, though, need some disposable income that can be spared if all does not go to plan.

As a member of a club you will learn more about finance and be able to invest modest sums routinely with less worry. By investing in this way, your risk is reduced and it can be a fun activity. It should also provide a savings scheme with a good rate of return.

Clubs range from pure fantasy/fun clubs to family clubs, international clubs, income clubs, specialty clubs, workplace clubs and clubs for growth. These are all run for different reasons and adopt different tactics to achieve their goals. You can even decide to invest as a virtual club so that you can learn the tricks of the trade without risking anything.

Understand Investment Clubs in a Day identifies and explains the processes involved in starting a club. This includes what to do, the legal considerations and how you should run your meetings effectively. It incorporates instructions on how to form a committee and advice on dealing with problems should they arise.

The book then examines what is involved in running a successful club, your level of commitment and what are the acceptable risks. It looks at how you recognise and deal with different member types and explains the need for delegation.

Once the club is up and running how will you make investment decisions? A list is included on where you can find relevant information and how you can interpret it to make informed decisions. This leads into suggestions for a balanced portfolio and discussions relating to investment type and associated risks.

Methods of monitoring your investments, once you have made that giant leap and bought something, and criteria for selling (including an examination of the factors that can affect share prices) are also discussed.

Of course it is important to be able to calculate personal and club net worth. The book shows you how to make valuations by using a simple calculator and unit based accounting system, which if carried out correctly makes auditing very easy.

It is worth re-stating that, if you are interested in learning more about shares and investment opportunities in a social setting that can be fun, educational and profitable, then an Investment Club is for you. Remember, above all else, you should enjoy the experience, learn, but laugh at the same time and do not take it all too seriously! You should be able to do this if you remember the golden rule: never invest money that you cannot afford to lose.

Chapter 1

What is an Investment Club?

INVESTMENT CLUBS are groups of people who are interested in share-ownership and are willing to meet regularly to discuss financial investments and pool (usually small amounts) of cash to invest in the stock market or other suitable investment opportunities. Members may work together, belong to the same professional organisation or just be friends from a social setting. The main idea is to combine your resources, (that's financial and knowledge based) while pursuing investment aims. Most people do not become hugely wealthy from Investment Clubs, but with some astute decisions and a measure of good luck can make very good returns. It is not a get rich scheme, but a long-term commitment leading towards increased personal wealth.

Investment Clubs have been around for decades now, but have gained in popularity in recent times. The first Clubs originated circa 1898 in Texas, USA. Since then Investment Clubs have gained in popularity around the world, particularly in Britain, France & Germany. It was in the 1950's when the concept transferred across the Atlantic to Britain.

There are currently hundreds of thousands of clubs around the world, reflecting a ten-fold increase over the last three years.

Total club assets are difficult to estimate accurately, but are thought to be in the hundreds of millions of pounds.

What are the Advantages of a Club?

If you are new to investing and are looking for a good way to get in on the act, a club provides the means for you to do just that:

- You may feel more comfortable investing as part of a group,
- Costs and risks are shared,
- Other people's ideas will help you to become a better investor.
- Individuals may bring with them sector specific experience, e.g. retail & fashion or sport & leisure.
- It could provide you with a new interest, a new dimension or a fun social outlet.

Education

Learning should be a major part of the club's operation. You will learn how to locate, assess, buy, monitor and sell shares. Becoming an active member of a club will provide opportunities to learn some of the methods and techniques involved in share trading.

To encourage this aspect you could decide to include an 'Education Officer' - someone whose role it is to promote education within the club. Club members should be invited to seek and explore new ideas and discuss investing issues. These may relate to some of the 'key' elements such as how to read annual reports and balance sheets, or even just dissemination of information from a good book by a well-known financial author. If you or any member of your group work for a large organisation, perhaps a talk from the company accountant on how to read company reports would be useful. A talk by a marketing executive may disclose how a company promotes itself and may yield some tips on how to dissect the glossy marketing speak. Then you can get at the bare bones of that company to make a more informed assessment. Even if you would not dream of reading the financial press at this stage, that could change as you gain more knowledge and interest.

There will inevitably be something beneficial to you simply from attending meetings (assuming it's not part of your day to day activities). You will see how to run a meeting, (chairperson), how to manage accounts, (treasurer), and how to organise the event, (club secretary). Then there is the invaluable experience of partaking, being assertive enough to have your say, being a part of a team with common goals. Then, assuming you make money, there is the satisfaction that you have been a part of the endeavours that have achieved that aim.

Sharing The Risk

Clubs utilise a shared decision making process and personal risk is reduced by making investments collectively.

Making investment decisions individually can be a very stressful business especially if your knowledge base on the subject is limited and it is all your own money that is being invested. By joining an Investment Club you can draw upon the skills and knowledge of your fellow members and collectively decide upon your investment route.

Rather than all of your money being risked in one or two purchases, you are now spreading the risk by investing in a greater number of companies in a variety of market sectors. Your fellow members are sharing the risk in both the decision making process and in the actual investment by taking advantage of shared information and a pooled fund, all of which reduce your personal exposure.

Many advisers suggest that you should not approach direct share holding unless you have of the order of £30,000 to invest. Even if you think this is excessive, it could take you a long time to amass enough funds to buy a reasonable quantity of shares. But pooling your money with other members of the Club will allow you to purchase reasonable numbers more quickly and more cheaply.

An Example of Pooling Resources

As an individual you may decide to buy shares in a particular company at £25 per share, but you only have £275 to spare. So you buy 10 shares with the dealing fees adding £25 to your outlay. Therefore the total cost of purchase is £275.

Now an Investment Club with 10 members may decide to buy 100 shares in the same company, again at £25 per share; this totals

£2500. The dealing fees remain the same at £25, which is only 1% of the total purchase price, giving a total outlay of £2525.

As an individual the same purchase of 10 shares cost you £275. Within the Investment Club it cost you a tenth of the £2525, which is £252.5, a saving of £22.50 just on that one transaction.

Pooling your money in this way allows diversification of your investment across a broad range of sectors (i.e. pharmaceuticals, engineering, utilities, etc) and by market (i.e. UK, Europe, USA, Asia, etc). This diversification is critical in the reduction of risk. It is always good practice to invest in different sectors. Thus, if one or more sectors perform badly your entire portfolio is not affected to the same degree. Other sectors you have invested in may perform well enough to counter the badly performing sectors.

An Example of Diversification

Two investment opportunities exist in Company A and Company B.

An individual only has £500 to invest and decides to buy 500 shares at £1 per share in Company A. It would not be economic to buy a smaller quantity in both Company A and Company B as dealing costs could amount to 10% of the available funds. An Investment Club has £1000 to invest and decides to buy 500 shares at £1 per share in Company A and 250 shares at £2 per share in Company B.

After the Investment Club and the individual have bought their shares, Company A's value drops by 50% and Company B's increases by 25%.

The individual's and the Investment Club's original £500 investment in Company A is now worth £250, (a 50% loss). The Investment Club's shares in Company B are now worth £625 - a profit of £125. Therefore the individual has lost £250, (50%), whereas the Investment Club has only lost £125, (25%).

Club Performance

Taking all Investment Clubs into account, and that includes those that make losses as well as profits, the average return on holdings are of the order 20% per annum*. This is a good return in comparison to bank deposits and government securities.

Investment Performance Comparison
% return per annum

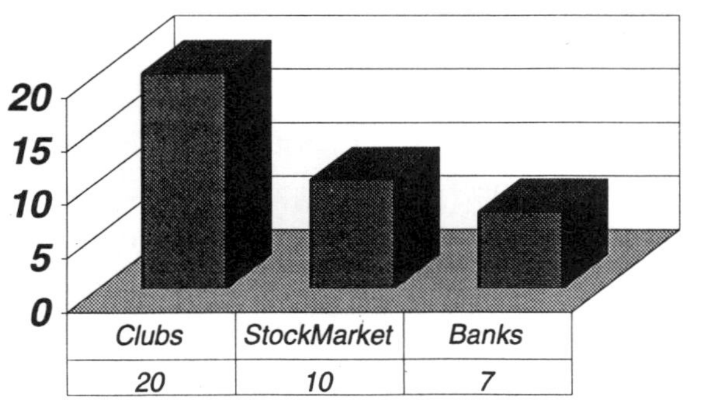

**The Source of the numeric data (directly related to clubs) as quoted above and throughout the book, is Proshare/Objective Research - August 2000. It was collected via a postal survey from a random sample of 1070 Investment Clubs.*

An interesting point to note is that all-female clubs make up to 30% profit, while all-male clubs only manage 22%. The ladies may take less risk and accept potentially lower, but more consistent, rewards.

The Social Side

Getting together with a group of like-minded people is one very good reason for joining an Investment Club, but is something that is often overlooked. Why not make it into an additional social element in your life? Many people, these days, have demanding routines, stressful jobs and limited opportunities for relaxation etc, so why not use this as a vehicle for some banter and friendly debate.

It is quite the opposite of locking yourselves away in isolation researching company data, accounts, spreadsheets and business pages. Instead you can turn making money into a lively and fun social event.

Take note, your intended members must be compatible socially, as well as in their investment philosophies. Finding the right people is key and should not be underestimated. Getting it right from the start will save you untold problems in the future. In Chapter 4, *Running the Club*, you'll be shown the potential member types and how to recognise them. It is only once they are in the club, however, that you can see their true character type. Until then you will need to make decisions based upon previous knowledge of their personality.

Summary

- ✔ Investment Clubs are a good vehicle for financial learning.

- ✔ Risk is shared through collective decision-making and investment.

- ✔ A Club thrives on pooled resources and you could regard money you invest through the Club as a 'Savings scheme'.

- ✔ Membership of an Investment Club can be fun.

Chapter 2

Types of Investment Club

THERE ARE Investment Clubs and there are Investment Clubs!

It is typical for a club to be run without any formal objectives other than for members to partake of financial wheeling and dealing, learning along the way and generally have a bit of fun buying shares. Whatever the club makes in terms of profit is an acceptable result and there is no direct dependency on the club being a financial success. This is the most usual type of club as it is easier to manage when there are no performance targets to meet.

Such a club may be set up as a short-term investment interest (say, two years) or for a longer-term (10 or more years). Either is acceptable, of course, but strategies should be aligned to match objectives.

Clubs with Fixed Objectives

Clubs can be run specifically to achieve a clear objective, e.g. a financial goal for a definitive event. In fact that may be their sole purpose for existence. Management of this type of club requires a different approach.

Always consider exactly what it is that you are investing for. Is it perhaps for a group trip to the next Olympic games, a new roof for the local church or to purchase a prized piece of land?

When an objective is identified a new club entirely could be set up to achieve the objectives. But in the same way that you can personally have different bank accounts and funds set up for various things in life, so you could set up an offshoot from an existing club.

The method to achieve your target is best explained in an example. Units are referred to in this example, but have not been discussed yet. The basic principle of unitising is explained in full in Chapter 8, *Calculating the Club Net Worth.*

Let's say you need to realise 500 units in four years, (48 months) to achieve your objectives. Based on a 25% return, then you will need to make payments over about 40 months, at ten units per month (40 Months x 10 units = 400 units). Presuming you can achieve a 25% return (100 units), you will achieve your target of 500 units within the timescale required, thus allowing for contingencies. This level of success will obviously require sensible investments and the usual measure of good luck.

Even if you weren't so successful, it should still be possible to outperform the banks and other similar investment opportunities and make the financial target that you have set yourself. If it is essential to meet your target and you are sure you want all the funds for your intended mission to come from the club, then increase the unit value paid in per month to perhaps 15 units. This will permit plenty of additional units even if the value of your stocks under-perform in practice. In fact that way you will still meet your target as long as you do not lose more than approximately 20%. For example, 40 Months x 15 units = 600 units. A loss of 20% is 120 units leaving you with 480 units, just under target and that's discounting the additional eight months contingency. Do remember, this is money that you would otherwise have spent on your objective, so it's a win-win situation.

Be aware that this type of Investment Club will require stricter running and monitoring than one that has no fixed goal or time period. Because this type of club has a fixed duration it is most important to realise any profits and minimise losses, e.g. cash in at the right time. Strategy will be critical and all members must agree completely. There can be no room for major disagreements. Perhaps more frequent club meetings may be necessary and certainly more vigilant study of the market and careful stock selection will be essential.

Usually re-investing the profit is the best option (using your money to make more money). However, as the duration of the club approaches its end, it may be wise to start moving some profits/sale money into more secure investments. These may be bank deposits or Government bonds - but try to find those which pay a decent rate of interest if the cash is going to be held there for some time.

Clubs for Growth

Resources are pooled each month to buy stock that will increase in value over time. The stock you choose will meet certain criteria (see Chapter 6 on *Making Investment Selections*) and could be classed as low to medium risk investments. By running a club dedicated to long term growth you will probably be excluding certain investment selections at the higher risk end e.g. Penny shares.

Income Clubs

Some Investment Clubs need to turn over a regular profit as they can be run to provide supplemental income. The setting up and running of this Investment Club, will be much the same as for one investing in growth stocks but they will differ in the investment strategy and tax planning. Tax planning makes it very complicated to run this type of club, and you will need to seek proper tax advice from the Inland Revenue/IRS or a qualified tax advisor.

If you, as an individual (i.e. not in your Investment Club), do not qualify for tax relief then all investment income will be taxable at the basic rate. There is no inflation indexing as there is for capital gains - and things get complicated because of varying individual members' tax situations.

Family Clubs

You may be part of a tight knit family group who communicate regularly and generally get on well. If this is the case you might like to share your financial interests. A family Investment Club is a perfectly good idea, as it may bring you together more regularly, other than just special occasions. When successful it would be great to spend some of the profit on a family get-together.

Workplace Clubs

A Workplace club would comprise of 'carefully selected ' work colleagues. Run it either within the building in your permitted break times or outside of normal working hours at an off-site venue. You could decide to invest in very specialist sectors that you have an intimate working knowledge of. If you know your own business, then it is quite likely that you have some idea of where the competition stands with their products. This can work, but does lead to a 'focused portfolio' and a lack of sector diversity.

Clubs Trading in Derivatives

Clubs have been known to deal only in derivatives, but it is not for the faint hearted. This involves betting on movements in stock markets via Options, Futures and other exotic instruments. Clearly this would not be a club for growth or income, but highly speculative in outlook. This type of trading is very risky.

Male and Female Clubs

There are maybe occasions when an Investment Club of all one sex is desirable. Possibly the exclusivity of an all-male or all-female club would appeal to you. You could even set up rival clubs to your partners and compete on a 'friendly' competitive basis.

International Clubs

As mentioned already one of the main driving forces of an Investment Club is the idea of getting together with a group of friends or work colleagues on a regular basis in a social setting. This then begs the question: is it possible to run an Investment Club with some or all members based overseas who are unable to commune regularly with the rest of the group? The answer is not a straightforward 'yes' or 'no' as there are several things to bear in mind.

The whole concept of an Investment Club is based on the need for regular discussion. If a member goes abroad only for a short period (perhaps for work reasons) then there is no real problem; if contact with the club is necessary then the telephone can be used. But if some or all the members of the club live abroad on a long term or permanent basis, it is a different issue altogether.

In theory it should be possible to run the club by telephone (perhaps with conference call facility) but for members living across different time zones this could be a problem. Another way of communication could be by e-mail.

Internet bulletin boards (specifically set up for your club members) may also provide a solution. With most or all members living abroad, the bulletin board could be the hub of communications.

The way to use it is to ask members to post all relevant information as they receive it. At the end of the week, (on a specified day), this information should be reviewed by club members. The same applies for proposals to buy or sell shares or any other club business.

You will need to make one person responsible for carrying out accepted proposals, e.g. to place the buy/sell orders and they should abide by the constitution. If a proposal to buy or sell has been made, set a time-scale for receipt of votes; perhaps seven days after the message has been posted. These votes need not be via the bulletin board, they could be via telephone; however use of the bulletin board records proposals and their outcomes historically.

On a more positive note there may be advantages to having club members living abroad. They will have more immediate access to information about companies based in the country they are living in. This is useful if you are thinking of investing internationally in part or perhaps exclusively.

Tax issues are of no great concern. Any profits are distributed to all the club members, (as for any normal club) and it is everyone's personal duty to refer any tax issues arising to the tax authority in the country where they reside.

So, in theory, running a successful International Investment Club is possible. It should be reiterated that some clubs can and do run successfully under these conditions.

Internationally Investing Clubs

An Investment Club that invests internationally is different from an International Club. Whereas an International Club consists of some or all members living overseas, International Investment Clubs are set up to invest exclusively in overseas stocks.

There are certain attractions to being a member of such a club, just as there is when buying into a specialist fund that only invests in certain markets, (e.g. Europe, USA, Asia, etc.) in that it helps you spread your risk further. So all your investments don't disappear if your home market takes a tumble across all sectors.

Fantasy Clubs

Fantasy Clubs do not invest for real. Theoretical portfolios and investments are made and monitored so that success or failure can be measured in terms of financial performance. One good reason to do this is to learn from the experience. There is nothing to lose, as there is no real fund in the first place - it is purely imaginary.

You will need to set a budget and decide the rules of the game to abide by. The rules may incorporate how frequently dealing is permitted, the dealing costs and a finite time whereby a result must be declared. This is a very good way to become familiar with trading. If you make mistakes it does not matter. What better way to practice the art of investing than as a 'virtual trader'? You may also want to incorporate this aspect into any other club format by running a fantasy competition with a small cash prize for the top trader.

There are a great many financial organisations on the Web, who promote this kind of fantasy trading with in-house competitions. The difference with such games (although there is no stake), is that there can be considerable prize money.

Summary

✔ It is typical for a club to be run without any formal objectives.

✔ A club for a fixed objective would have a finite life and could be new or an offshoot of an existing club.

✔ There may be difficulties with International Clubs, but they are not insurmountable.

✔ Income clubs can be complex to administer.

✔ A 'Fantasy Club' where trades are imaginary can familiarise you with share trading.

✔ Workplace Clubs biased towards a specific sector can be successful but are susceptible to sector variation through a lack of diversity.

Chapter 3

Starting an Investment Club

THE PROCESSES involved in starting a club and the correct sequence of events will be explained here. There are some specific steps you will need to take to form a club, but the whole process is straightforward. You could actually get one up and running within a week or so, but in reality it's more likely to be a month or two from initial discussion to a time when you are ready and able to make a first purchase.

What is it that prompts someone to start a club? Usually a club comes into being because acquaintances find that they have a common interest in finance and in investing in shares. They realise that there are benefits from investing as a collective and decide to get together.

Is there a good time to start one?

There are no hard and fast rules when it would be better or less beneficial to start a club. If the market is low, it may well present buying opportunities, but you do have to be careful and very selective. If the markets have been at a low for quite some time, say over a year, then unless a recession is looming there is a good chance that the market may turn around soon.

The markets often display regular characteristics. For example towards the year end there is often some increase in volume and a bullish outlook. This outlook will often survive until approximately the end of April. Then the well known saying comes to mind, "sell in May and stay away". Typically, volumes are low and trading is reduced in the summer months while everyone is on vacation. Prices do not tend to move much and remain relatively static. Then as autumn approaches, things begin to pick up and volumes increase taking us back to the start of the market cycle.

This trend, although repeated more often than not when analysing historical data, cannot be relied upon to make your buying/selling decisions or when to start a club, but it may help your strategy.

Looking for Members

Find other people who would be interested with broadly the same aims and investment strategy and who would be supportive of the intended means to achieve club objectives.

Ask around, talk to friends and colleagues and find out if they are interested in the idea. You do not need to find all potential members yourself as you can mention the idea to a few friends who will in turn approach some of their friends who they think will be suitable to join. You will soon find that there is more than enough interest. It might be good to encompass people with a range of interests, experiences and perspectives, as broad-ranging knowledge is useful.

Identify three volunteers to initially form a small nucleus of 'key' members. This group could then scrutinise potential members for suitability and take the reins in the early stages.

Now, consider who and how many you will invite to join. Then once you have your select group of key persons and a large enough group interested, collate a list of interested parties, record their names and addresses and send out invitations to a preliminary meeting. In the letter inviting potential members, state clearly the venue, date and time and ask them to confirm their attendance. Perhaps, add a return slip, requesting a response from those who cannot make it but would still like to be kept informed of events. Allow a reasonable period between invitation and the proposed date of the meeting.

There may or may not be a constitution or draft rules at this point, however, if there are any 'conceptual notes' for a constitution or ideas for rules, these should accompany the letter of invitation. You can refer to the sample constitution in Appendix 2 and extract relevant aspects for your own use.

The Preliminary Meeting

The preliminary meeting will not be an official meeting of the proposed club, but will simply be an informal discussion where all interested parties get together to debate how the club might be run. It is very important to give some thought to the content of your meeting beforehand as you will want to appear professional and give a good account of yourself. The range of discussion should cover all facets of a club's operation. It will be necessary to install a chairperson who would ideally be able to give a short presentation about Investment Clubs and their virtues, etc. Also 'volunteer' somebody to take notes. These notes can then be typed up and distributed after the meeting.

At this preliminary meeting talk about what is involved in a being part of a club and the level of commitment expected. Some items to consider and discuss might be:-

- Do you have enough in common? Do you think you would all get along together?

- How would the club be organised and run? - Are there any ideas for a constitution?

- How serious are the invitees about forming a club? Are they prepared for the commitment?

- What is an acceptable monthly payment? Discuss what would be a preferred method of payment.

- Is there strong opinion on the issue of membership size, e.g. will some form of limit be preferred?

Discuss these issues, gauge opinion and then decide how many and who specifically you will invite to join. This is of course a selection process, but a necessary one.

What Size of Membership?

The size of club membership is important and requires careful thought. With too many members you may find that it is difficult to reach any kind of decision and there will undoubtedly be conflicts of opinion surfacing from time to time.

You will also need to bear in mind that 20 is a legal upper limit if your club is to be set up as an equal partnership. If it is bigger than this, i.e. greater than twenty members, there are complications to consider and you would need to register as a formal company.

The size of the club is for you to decide; many start out with 10 members as it seems logical for ease of calculations and enough to collect sufficient funds in just a few months to enable a first buy. One noteworthy benefit of a smaller membership is that it permits a smoother, faster and less bureaucratic decision making processes.

The Inaugural meeting

The Inaugural meeting is the first formal meeting of the club where many of the practical aspects necessary to run the club are decided. Appendix 1 gives an example of what might form the basis of an agenda for the inaugural meeting.

This agenda is optional and you could put off selecting a name for the club until the second meeting, (meanwhile get people thinking about this, perhaps to bring along suggestions to the next meeting). Many clubs name themselves after their favourite meeting place or a variation on the name of their workplace.

At this stage take any written or verbal apologies for absence and take note of the names for recording in the minutes of the meeting.

Election of Officers

Early on in the meeting be sure to elect officers. This is done by voting with a show of hands and is achieved by a simple majority of members attending the meeting. You will need to decide on a chairperson, treasurer and secretary. Also any other roles that you might decide on, such as a social secretary, education officer etc; these can be created at your discretion.

The chairperson should have some knowledge of the stock market and be able to control meetings and keep everyone enthusiastic while maintaining order and a sense of decorum. Ideally this person should be confident, possess some leadership skills and be able to command respect.

The Treasurer's job will be to set up the club's bank account and share-dealing account, also to do the book-keeping, keep financial records, produce monthly and annual reports and deal with any tax issues should you be so successful as to warrant this concern.

The role of club secretary is not to be underestimated, there is plenty to do and it is without doubt a challenging and important role. The Secretary's duties include arranging meetings, producing an agenda and taking minutes, helping with membership administration and providing back up to the chairperson and the treasurer.

All these positions can be demanding and are key to the club's operation. You should remember to share the responsibility and delegate tasks occasionally, perhaps to a deputy. It is also worth appointing deputies for each of these key roles to cover for eventualities, e.g. absence, departures etc. They should also be asked to undertake the regular duties of the officer from time to time to ensure familiarity. Officers will need to resign before the AGM, (Annual General Meeting) but are eligible for re-election. Once you have officers who can take control of the proceedings - you're in business. Allow the chairperson to direct the meeting from here onwards.

Discuss the Constitution

Be sure to set out the club's constitution, (that is the rules by which the club is governed), and discuss members likes/dislikes. Also be prepared to compromise and work towards a mutually acceptable document. You may want to use a standard document for this; see Appendix 2.

Ask the membership for approval of the draft constitution. Ensure there is no ambiguity and that it covers voting rights etc. Will you want 'one member one vote' or will you prefer a scheme which gives additional say to members who have a bigger percentage stake in the club? These are operational rules that must be decided upon, employed and obeyed.

Once the constitution is finalised and all the formalities have been decided, make sure copies are distributed and signed by all those who have agreed to join. However, this may have to wait until the next meeting if you have agreed any changes to the original document.

Your constitution should state what is required for a quorum. A quorum is the minimum number of members required to make formal decisions. It should be a fixed number of the membership and can be adjusted based upon total size. For example, if the club has ten members, then 6 from 10 might be regarded as quorate (there are a qualifying number of members present). If the club has 18 members, you might want 12 members present to be quorate. As a guideline, a quorum should comprise roughly two thirds of the membership.

If a meeting is non-quorate, then it simply means there is less than the prescribed number of members present for a quorum and no decisions that affect the other member's can be made.

Note, the draft constitution points will not be written in tablets of stone and can be altered later. Although strictly speaking once the club is up-and-running changes should only be made at a quorate Extraordinary or Annual General Meetings. You should send a copy of your constitution to your broker and the bank where your account is held. The bank may also ask to see copies of minutes of meetings.

Stockbrokers

At this stage of the meeting it would be wise to discuss stockbrokers and move towards appointing or at least agreeing upon one. Ask members for preferences, but be prepared to supply information in the event that they have not done their homework.

Some brokers offer tailor-made services for Investment Clubs, which are a very useful and a highly recommended feature. These will generally provide the lowest cost deals available.

You can open an account with a stockbroker by depositing some money or shares; they will advise what they need and how to go about it. It is then necessary in most cases to pass identity/credit checks, but this is usually a formality. Transactions are carried out by telephone, placing orders via the Internet or by post.

It is advisable to form a basic agreement between your club and the broker stating terms and conditions (the broker should be able to supply something upon request). Ensure all members sign this agreement and keep a filed copy for the records.

Types of shareholding

At this point it is a good idea to highlight the types of share holding available and the advantages/disadvantages of each. From experience we would recommend a 'nominee' holding - these are becoming much more popular as the shares you buy are automatically registered in the stockbrokers name, but on your behalf. This eliminates the need for some paperwork.

The down side of nominee holdings is that they do not always lead to the usual shareholder perks. For example you will need to request information such as Annual Reports, details of AGMs, EGMs, etc. When you have a traditional share holding it is your name that the company has registered as owner of the shares, hence you get everything mailed directly to you as it becomes available. You can, however, choose to have real printed share certificates, but these take time to generate and register. Also when you sell you will need to send the certificates with a signed transfer form.

You could decide to take the approach of trustees, but this may be less than ideal in certain scenarios. This is an alternative where you can appoint two or three club members as trustees and register your shares in their names. The problem with this approach is that if one of the trustees leaves, each investment registered with that person's name will have to be altered and re-registered accordingly using a stock transfer form. This incurs stamp duty at 0.5% and possibly a registration fee as well. The trustee approach is probably best suited to a club with proven stability and stocks purchased for long term growth.

Club Start up Funds

It is usual for Investment Clubs to ask for an initial membership fee, which boosts funds at the start. This will enable shares to be bought fairly quickly, thus satisfying everyone's enthusiasm, which will be high at the outset.

Subscriptions and Accounts

The level of the monthly contribution will depend on the wealth of the membership. It is important to always retain the fun element, so you should keep to a small monthly subscription. Most clubs find it necessary to compromise with the level of payments, usually deferring to the person demanding the lowest level of payment, based upon what they could afford.

Obviously the Club will need to open a bank account to accommodate the new funds. It will be necessary to obtain the relevant forms to set-up a 'treasurer' account; these will be made available on request, just telephone the bank. The account you open must be set up in the name of the club and the bank must be given written confirmation, with specimen signatures of those entitled to draw cheques.

A Treasurer's account is ideal for Investment Clubs as it comes with a cheque book, a paying-in book and sometimes the first ten transactions in a month are for free. You should look for this kind of deal.

Most Clubs nominate three officers as signatories; typically allowing any two from three to sign cheques. This is not just for security reasons, it is to comply with banking rules. As mentioned earlier, do not forget to supply detail of the club's constitution and make up of the membership, especially the officers, to the bank. Once you have completed all the paperwork, an account sort code and account number will be allocated in the club's chosen name.

Once an account is fully functional, the simplest way to collect funds from each member is to ask them to set up a standing order direct to the club's bank account.

Additional Contributions

It is possible to make additional contributions and buy more units in the club, (if your constitution permits it). You could choose to buy twice as much or any multiple of the normal level of payment. The constitution in these instances is key. If individuals buy twice as many units as another they might want twice as much influence in decision-making processes, e.g. two votes.

Non Payment of Contributions

This can be a difficult area to tackle. What if a member does not pay? If it is just a 'one off' then they can be approached, (by the treasurer usually) to enquire if there is a good reason. If there is, then they can make amends with a top-up payment and undertaking to maintain regular payments from then on.

If there are other reasons for non-payment, they should be asked if they would like to remain a member of the club. If the answer is, "Yes" you can offer to suspend their units. This means that they need not pay in any more contributions, but their personal worth increases only in line with the performance of the club, e.g. as the unit value increases.

Alternatively they may want to leave the club for personal or financial reasons. If they do then proceed to calculate their personal worth at an agreed time (snapshot) and plan to make a pay out in due course; it is usual to give three months notice. The means to calculate club and personal worth is covered in detail in Chapter 8.

Where to hold Club Meetings

You will need to decide on the frequency of meetings and the venue(s). Most Investment Clubs meet once a month with dates fixed well in advance. Where should you meet? If you are linked via a business interest it will probably be best kept outside the workplace (unless you have specifically chosen to operate that way with your company's blessing).

Otherwise resist the temptation to use the 'tools of the trade' at your workplace, that way nothing can be implied regards the impact of activities on your efficiency. Web monitoring at the workplace is now legal and easily carried out with low cost solutions.

A meeting place should be somewhere that everybody is comfortable with. An obvious one is a pub or bar, especially in winter, with a roaring fire, a packet of crisps/chips and a couple of beers or a glass of wine to wash it down. This then provides an amiable setting in which to discuss affairs, although the degree of privacy is, of course, in question. If you want solitude, why not meet in each other's homes on a rota basis?

If you do have meetings in member's homes, agree strict rules about hospitality so that everyone knows what is expected of them. It is usual to meet at least once a month to keep on top of affairs and actively monitor stock values etc.

Making Decisions at Meetings

All investment decisions should be taken at quorate meetings (i.e. a certain number of the club members should be present). By now you will be aware of the importance of a club's constitution.

As part of that constitution you will have selected what your decision making process entails, e.g. should the meeting be quorate, should a majority decision be required, are proxy votes to be included, etc.

The Secretary should draw up an agenda and send out an invitation asking for all club members to attend. In drawing up the agenda the Secretary should ask club members for proposals including the names of companies to be discussed as potential investments. At the meeting the Secretary should assess if the meeting is quorate, if it is then the meeting goes ahead and the chairperson directs the meeting through the agenda. If it is not, then the meeting can either be cancelled and rescheduled or can proceed but no formal decisions can be accepted as a result.

Minutes can be taken by any elected person but it is usually the Secretary's task to do this. An example Agenda (for an Ordinary meeting) is given in Appendix 3.

Good management of a meeting involves keeping to a set time and agenda. It is no good scheduling an hour for the meeting and have fifty companies to review during that hour. Time is at a premium so keep the agenda sensible. Experience suggests that on occasions it is difficult getting through one or two tips per hour. Debate can start over the smallest of issues and although this is healthy, it is critical for the Chairperson to keep control of the debate and keep everyone to the point. If time does not permit the discussion of all proposals then another meeting may be necessary. It is usual to vote on a proposal with a show of hands and a majority of the club membership carries the vote, unless your constitution states a majority of those in attendance.

Dealing with dissenters and disagreements

There is a thin line between healthy debate and disagreement. Often you will find that there is a need to be diplomatic. In some instances where problems arise, you will need to rely on the chairperson to bring matters under control. Everyday disagreements are not in themselves problematic, but what you must avoid is a full-scale walkout. Perhaps even agree to disagree.

Legal Considerations

Do not neglect the legal formalities of setting up the club. What are they? You might like to consider these; are you set up as an equal partnership, have you taken care of the tax implications and is your membership size suitable? As a club of less than 20 members you will be a partnership which cuts out the expense of forming a limited company and the possible problems of corporation tax.

However well you know your membership be sure that no one person has overall financial control. It is unlikely that anyone will disappear with the funds, but do make sure they cannot. The way to do this is to ensure that at least two people, usually the officers, have to sign to authorise financial transactions. You should pursue this in all instances even if your club comprises solely family members. Draw up a formal contract and ensure all members sign it, then if anything goes wrong it ensures you are protected by the terms and conditions.

Taxation will only become an issue if you exceed your personal capital gains allowance. For most this will not be a problem. You can find out what the existing threshold is by calling your local tax office.

In the UK, you should note that members cannot be paid for financial advice under the rules of the Financial Services Act, 1986.

Summary

✔ There are no hard and fast rules about when it may be best to start a club.

✔ Form a select group of two or three 'key players' to make initial decisions.

✔ Set a target size for membership that is less than 20; exactly10 is ideal.

✔ Arrange a preliminary meeting.

- ✔ Implement a comprehensive constitution and elect officers.
- ✔ Be sure there are no ambiguities in the constitution and that it covers voting rights.
- ✔ Set up a bank account for collection of funds.
- ✔ Select a stockbroker to suit your needs.
- ✔ Discuss club funds, including initial and additional contributions and non-payment of contributions.
- ✔ Discuss and decide upon a suitable venue to hold meetings.
- ✔ Do ensure that you have not neglected the legalities and that you are protected.

Chapter 4

Running the Club

THIS CHAPTER explores best practice in the running of and administration of your club. There are some key factors you need to employ and maintain to ensure continued success.

Identifying Your Aims

The main aims are likely to be learning about shares and other investment opportunities and making money. However there are many different approaches you may take.

You may be interested in investing in certain sectors, perhaps for steady growth or income, or you may wish to concentrate on some high-risk selections. Having some idea of your specific aims will provide a focus to your Investment Club and provide the foundation of its success.

What are your Commitments?

If you are an elected officer then you will need to devote some time to the activity, perhaps two - four hours per month to keep on top of the administration. As an ordinary club member it will be your 'informal duty' to watch out for good potential buys, partake of meeting discussions and occasionally help with any tasks delegated to you.

In an ideal world all club members would take it in turns to research and report on promising companies that may prove worthy investments or seek further information on those that are already held by the club. Then everybody can bring something to the portfolio. It is also a good thing if members track one or two shares as future options for purchase; someone in the club who is perhaps keener than the rest might need to allocate prospective companies.

All members should be encouraged to seek financial information/data and be as proactive as they feel comfortable. That should apply to all aspects of the club's operation in support of the officers.

Be prepared to give time freely within your personal limitations. A monthly meeting typically takes between one and three hours and research prior to the meeting could be of the order two to six hours per month.

Therefore you are typically looking at a total of between three and nine hours per month.

Subscriptions

It is important that subscriptions are paid on time. This should be straightforward, with the option to set up a standing order to the club's account for a fixed sum on a specific day/date each month.

The treasurer can then report the new balance and any transactions at the monthly meeting.

To cover the club's administration costs you may wish to charge a small levy in addition to the monthly contribution. Any surplus cash could be used to fund a social event or be put back into club funds.

There is nothing worse than someone who has to be repeatedly asked for their contributions. It is bad practice not to pay on time and worse still to miss a payment without informing the treasurer. This kind of behaviour can lead to discord within the club, something you clearly want to avoid. Non payments need to be tackled as soon as possible.

If you are the treasurer and are charged with the task of pursuing payments, try to be diplomatic and find out if a payment has been missed with good reason. You will then need to decide which course of action to take.

There are two options. Offer to suspend the member's payments, (if it's a financial problem) or ask them if they want to leave the club for personal or financial reasons.

Club Etiquette

It is good etiquette to send your apologies to the club secretary if you are unable to attend a meeting. This is then recorded and you are not considered to simply have forgotten or lost interest. Avoid arguments at all costs and try to be positive in your outlook and give other members' ideas due consideration.

Do

- Send apologies to the club secretary prior to a meeting if you cannot attend (this is then recorded and you are not considered to have forgotten or lost interest).
- Avoid Arguments at all cost as this can lead to discord.
- Give other member's ideas due consideration - try to be positive in your outlook.
- Always be courteous - try to create a friendly environment where everyone feels at ease.
- Respect your fellow members.
- Be punctual - arrive promptly and keep to time.
- Abide by the constitution.
- Fulfil your financial obligations - ensure payments are made regularly and efficiently.

Don'ts

- Do not argue with your fellow members.
- Do not neglect your duties as basic commitments - pull your weight in all aspects.
- Do not miss payments, (this causes the treasurer some consternation).
- Never speak over others or interrupt when they are having their say as invited by the chairperson.
- Do not domineer - be a part of the team, remember you are merely one member in an Organisation.
- Do not bad mouth other members - nobody likes a backstabber, keep opinions to yourself.

Fun

Your ultimate goal should be to have fun; try not to lose sight of that. Meetings should be enjoyable events with an interjection of humour at suitable opportunities.

If you are enjoying the social side, the banter and debate, the seeking of new ideas for investments and you are getting a buzz from it all regardless of financial performance, then your club is a success. If you are making money as well, then that is the icing on the cake.

Keeping The Club Fresh and Successful

It is vitally important to add variety to prevent proceedings from becoming stale and uninspiring.

There are a number of techniques that can be used to maintain and stimulate interest. These include varying the venue, changing the format for meetings and occasionally using club funds in some novel way.

If morale is flagging for any reason, then this is when the club's activities need bolstering with a field trip, a guest speaker or similar. Something out of the norm to liven things up is needed. Why not have an off-topic discussion or debate, something ideally of a light-hearted nature, this can help to stimulate or rekindle interest. You may want to revise the constitution, for example, regarding the frequency of meetings.

Meeting Places

Try meeting at different locations - for example pubs/bars or a similar social venue. Take into account the majority's preference and be prepared to compromise. Certainly consider running some of the meetings, such as an Extraordinary General Meeting or Annual General Meeting at a pub/bar, which offers a good choice of cuisine. Always ask yourself if the venue is appropriate - perhaps it's too noisy, lacks atmosphere or is not suited to formal meetings.

Annual Review Meetings

You should plan to hold an 'Annual review meeting' to reassess share purchases and sales that you've made throughout the year. You can also discuss what you've learned from these transactions, e.g. were they the right decisions? How was the timing? Can this experience lead to improvements such as better research?

Also take the opportunity to review any objectives. It may be necessary to change your objectives in the light of economic changes and market pressures etc. Possibly your plans for the club may have altered or been modified with time.

Regular Accounting

Implement a valuation day, whereby at a designated date each month the club net worth is calculated. Get the bank to send monthly statements to coincide with this date, as it will make reconciliation easier.

Do not forget to conduct an annual review (audit) of the accounts. This will need to be a formal, in-depth assessment of the accounts such that profit/loss information can be produced for tax declaration purposes.

Reasons for Failure

Most research shows that few clubs actually make it past a couple of years. The reasons are many and varied, as are the *possible solutions.*

If the Club's asset values fall, members may lose interest

If the clubs asset value continues to fall during its lifetime this can affect morale and members will begin to question their involvement. No one wants to see their investment lose money regardless of how much fun their involvement in a club can be. Members may lose interest more quickly during a market that is falling and special countermeasures are needed.

During a falling market, choose your share purchases very carefully. There may be sound financial reasons for buying at these times. However, it may be the one time when it would be better to stock-pile cash then at least members will see the club net worth increasing. Remind members that they should be prepared to take the rough with the smooth and always continue to invest regardless of market conditions; (with the odd exception if market conditions are very poor). Careful deployment of distractions, (fun aspects), at meetings may help to alleviate the problem.

There is a lack of clear objectives

A club without clear objectives is like a ship without a rudder, direction-less. Your objectives should be defined in the early days of the club and refined over time.

Define, know and follow your objectives. Do not lose sight of what it is that you have set out to achieve. Make sure your targets are realistic.

Meetings are badly planned and run

Meetings at an inappropriate time of day are prone to failure. Poor timekeeping and overlong meetings can be a problem.

Ensure the venue is acceptable to all, i.e. it is not too noisy, smoky, and dingy or lacks atmosphere. Be sure to get the timing correct; in the evening, after a hard day's work may not be ideal. Also choose an acceptable venue, with a well-structured agenda, paying particular attention to timekeeping. Often, and this is a recommendation, short direct sessions may be best as people will be more focused and attentive. Take breaks from the main discussion from time to time. Do not try to do it all in one session, there is always another day.

There is a lack of financial awareness

If members fail to gain sufficient financial knowledge, on financial matters, mistakes can be made in stock selection. This can also induce errors in the timing and quantities of share purchases.

Be sure to actually gain some basic knowledge on investing and incorporate this learning aspect into your meetings. Perhaps employ a 'five minute' focus where a member can bring a topic to present. Make it into a fun thing by awarding a prize for the best presentation.

There is a lack of leadership

A lack of leadership may lead to unproductive meetings and general operation of the club.

You will need one or more people to direct the club and ideally they should command respect, be authoritative and possess good communication skills. Typically the leader, or leaders, will be elected officers.

Under-delegation is prevalent

Failure to delegate suitably will inevitably lead to some members doing more work than others. This is okay while they are happy with that scenario, but it can lead to resentment of others who appear to be getting a free ride.

Do delegate all tasks equally within the club where possible.

There is insufficient commitment shown

Inadequate commitment can affect all aspects of the club's operation, such as missed buying opportunities, lack of research, etc. These may affect the clubs objectives and its raison d'être.

Members need to realise the required levels of commitment and not only that, but be prepared to contribute both regularly and effectively.

Members take it all much too seriously

If members take proceedings too seriously, there is no room for the fun element - one of the main reasons for being in a club. It can stifle productive debate, as some members may feel intimidated.

You could choose to operate a yellow and red card based system, similar to football as a mechanism for punishment. A yellow card would mean a first warning and would warrant a mandatory five-minute silence. A red card means the member is expelled for the remaining duration of the meeting. Alternatively employ an obligatory moneybox penalty and, when a serious comment is made, apply a fixed price fine.

It is important to retain the fun element and not get too serious. Anyone who takes proceedings too seriously should be booted out, or at least reprimanded!

Jargon is used much too regularly

Too much jargon is unnecessary, is a turn off and those that use it are often out to impress.

Ask everyone to avoid jargon except where essential.

Domineering members take control

Domineering members can disrupt meetings and create a bad atmosphere.

Your chairperson must be assertive, control the meeting and permit everybody to take part.

There are large differences of opinion

If differences of opinion exist then it may be difficult to agree on investment strategy and heated arguments may ensue.

You cannot avoid differences of opinion so be prepared to compromise and act in the best interests of the club. That's not meant to suggest that you always back down, but at least adopt a constructive outlook. It's often better to win the war, not just the battle.

There are too many clashes of personality

Just as in life, you are likely to end up with a whole plethora of different character types and this may lead to personality clashes and dislikes which can be very bad for the club.

Consider your member types and what motivates them. Consult the section, below, on common breeds and you may recognise what makes these individuals tick. This can be very positive in dealing with them if you understand their motivation.

Member Types

It is import to choose members of your club very carefully and hopefully end up with a club of like-minds. Unfortunately the reality is (or can be) very different. And once your club is up and running, only then do you see the different investment character-types in their true light. For example prospective club members who proclaimed they were keen on Penny shares may change their mind once the reality of putting up their own hard-earned cash hits home. Others may display personality traits that you had never seen before or even suspected.

So it is important to recognise different character types as the club goes along and learn how to live with them. Remember you are aiming for one big happy family within the club.

There are some very clear 'common breeds' amongst a typical club's membership. There are individuals that can easily be classified based on their behaviour and personality. These common breeds can be further classified as either harmless or dangerous.

Harmless Types

The Fence-Sitter is unable to become fully committed or express a personal opinion. He/she is easily swayed either way depending upon who is winning the debate. The Fence Sitter is a good candidate for lobbying should the need arise.

The Sleeper has a passing interest and they come alive on limited occasions, have their say, then doze off again. Would be keen if they could muster the interest and master the subject, but they cannot quite get there. One annoying facet of the sleeper is that they usually wake up and become involved just when you do not expect them to e.g. when you are trying to push for that little stock you've fancied for sometime and are on the verge of securing a club decision. Suddenly the sleeper is in the thick of the action and swaying the club decision the other way. You would not mind this if the sleeper was involved regularly in debate but sporadic involvement can become annoying.

The only way around this is to encourage the sleeper to be more active for longer periods of time. If they do get involved in a particular issue ask them to go away and provide some documented research on the topic. This may encourage more active participation in the future.

The Conservative, means well, but stifles activities and tends to be too timid and cautious regarding both buys and sells. The conservative annoys the gung-ho types enormously. This type is fine if the entire group is conservative in their stock picking but in reality this is usually not the case. Sometimes, though, it is good to have some conservative opinion within a group to provide balance and they can be useful in offsetting the gung-ho types.

Moaners are never content and always griping. This member can affect meeting morale, as they tend to be pessimistic in nature. Try to instill a more optimistic outlook; counter their vocal negativity at every opportunity. This will offset their tales of woe and they may even come round to your way of thinking if you are persistent.

Pedantic Types are the people that can quote chapter and verse. They will know the club's constitution like the back of their hand and will take every opportunity to recite it. This makes them feel good. They will question every decision and deal. If you allow them to reign, you will never get anything done. Obviously, give them their moment as, what they have to say is accurate, but do not let them go too far - ask them to be concise and eliminate boorish detail.

Dangerous varieties

With the **Gung-Ho** anything goes, 'who needs research'! They are likely to talk up a share if they have a personal (often unjustified) preference for it.

Do not knock the gung-ho types. Although they can talk forever and a day on the upsides of a stock - they may just be right. Usually you find that they are very active researchers and know the share well. But, also, do not take everything they say as gospel - they can gloss over the negative in favour of the positive side of a stock, so remember to do your own research on their picks as well. These characters can provide a lot of the activity and fun element to the club. Do not discourage them unless you have to.

It's my Party is the dominator, apt to say, "do it my way, I know best"! More than one of these in a single club will inevitably lead to clashes and confrontations. One is just about acceptable in a club, two or more and it's a disaster waiting to happen. The whole concept of the club is based on group involvement - if any member/members start dominating and harassing others into decisions, then the fabric of the club will disintegrate.

The Baby is the type that will want everything done their way and will get upset if decisions go against their beliefs. They may not openly rebel, but are more likely to conspire against the perpetrators in office corridors or at the coffee machine.

They will need to be spoon-fed snippets of information, as they often do not see the bigger picture. Occasionally they need to be pacified and spoken to in a very tactful manner. These types are not always easy to spot initially, although they always show themselves before too long. Treat them with caution they can be disruptive.

Show-offs use an awful lot of jargon, without really knowing what they are talking about. They like the sound of their own voice and need to be restrained (this could be tricky, but can be achieved through assertive chairing of the meetings). Do, however, give them occasion to speak as you would do for other members, but you must strike a balance.

The Scrooge is nervous of spending money and therefore difficult to persuade to vote for a share purchase. You have to find out if this character is really happy contributing to the club and whether they can, or perhaps more importantly if they want to, afford it. There is no positive element in this character unless you recognise other redeeming features. They really defeat two of the main purposes of the club, to invest freely from a pooled resource and to have fun!

Learning to Live with Others

If you can understand the psychology behind what motivates individuals, then you are immediately at an advantage and your level of tolerance will be increased. Make sure you do not take the running of the club too seriously and resist the temptation to get carried away with bureaucracy. Take opportunities to inject humour - a degree of light-heartedness always helps!

Winding up the Club

This is one of the least inspiring aspects of running a club, but none the less an essential chore. Again the practical aspect falls into the lap of the treasurer, but it is straightforward.

All you need to do is decide on a date when you will sell all stocks held. Admittedly some will be up in value and some will be down with others mid-price. If you do sell on a specified date there is at least a defined procedure and the agony is not prolonged.

At the agree date, sell all. When the proceeds of these sales come in add them to any surplus funds in the bank and you now have a total value. If there are any other assets held by the club they will need to be sold and added to the total. Also be sure that no money is still owed to the club. A possible complication can arise if dividends are paid directly into the club's account (these may arrive after the closing calculations).

Simply calculate the total numbers of units held by all club members and divide this number of units into the cash sum. This will give you a single unit value, which can be multiplied by the number of units each member holds. You then have a figure for each member's pay off. If you have done your sums correctly, the amount you pay out will equal the cash total held. The result should be a zero balance, at which point you can proceed to close all the accounts by writing to the appropriate bodies concerned. Note that once you have a total club worth resulting from the sale of all assets you then need to calculate the unit value.

Alternative

Another option to consider is to offer the share holdings to club members who have personal investing interests outside of the club. There might be members who would like the opportunity to buy the shares from the club, particularly if the share was 'their baby' in the first place. This will need to be at the current market value with the valuation date and time agreed in advance. The total sale cost should include any transfer fees, e.g. if there is a cost for transferring the stock from the club to the individual's sole name. At least this way some members benefit from the closure of the club.

Summary

- ✔ Be clear in your aims.
- ✔ Make everyone aware that they will need to invest some time in their club.
- ✔ Encourage members to make payments on time.
- ✔ Keep up-to-date with the accounts.
- ✔ Delegate duties on occasions to share workload and so that others can gain experience.
- ✔ Observe good etiquette.
- ✔ Boost morale wherever possible and maintain the fun element.
- ✔ Recognise and learn to live with the other members.
- ✔ It is a fairly straightforward task to wind up a club, especially if operating a unit based scheme.
- ✔ You can employ an alternative to selling all shares by transferring them to other members, in the form of buyouts.

Chapter 5

Joining an Existing Club

YOU CAN JOIN a club at any time. The basic mechanism will involve an approval from the club's existing members (at a formal meeting) and a 'buy in'.

Vacancies

Established clubs will occasionally have vacancies for new members due to a host of reasons. Members may leave as they need to realise their investment for personal reasons or they may be leaving the activity or workplace that unites the group. Or perhaps they simply have other ideas they wish to pursue. Having said that, opportunities to join a club are hard to come by, as most clubs will have friends they would propose or there may even be a waiting list.

Where can you find a Club?

You can locate clubs and other people willing to join a club by using some of the financial web sites that provide bulletin boards or discussion forums. However, the bias on these is 'National' and the chances of you finding someone suitable in the same town or locality can be limited.

Most clubs are usually formed by groups of friends or work colleagues - in fact 77% of all clubs are formed from these two groups. It is because these clubs comprise mainly friends and colleagues that they prefer anonymity. In some cases they will be wary about introducing strangers into their group as money is involved.

However, there are some options available to enable you to find a club. You can locate a club in cyberspace; you could even join a cyberspace club without ever coming face to face with other members. You can employ the Internet and make good use of search engines with appropriate key words. In this way you will be able to access Investment Club lists and club directories.

Ask around at your place of work; your co-workers may already be involved in running clubs. You might be surprised to find that there are such clubs in existence, perhaps even well established.

Try placing an advertisement in local newspapers, perhaps using a box number so you can check responses suitably without supplying any personal detail.

This may seem like limited information on the subject of how to find a club, but the fact is, it seems like an easy thing to do, when in reality it is not. Perhaps you'd be better off starting your own club...

What to look for when joining a Club

If you do find a club that looks worth joining you should first consider these items:

Would you get on with the other members? What sort of characters are they? (See member types earlier in the text). Assess if the membership have the right mix of qualities - are they too quiet or too brash, are they about the right age and do they appear friendly and welcoming? Is their thinking in line with your own on investment strategy and are the regular contributions about right for you?

If all is in order and the club seems reasonably aligned to your principles/preferences, then why not give it a go. A good club should be able to furnish you with a formal constitution and some form of information regards investment strategy including stock selection processes, monitoring and buy/sell criteria.

How long has the club been established and how successful has it been? To be honest all the good textbooks on investments always mention the fact that past performance should never be taken as a guide to future performance. But in reality it is often the biggest clue you have to how a club has been managed, so you should look at the club's recorded. What have they invested in and how do the returns look? Do your own research too and do not necessarily rely on what the club members tell you.

Request a look at the club accounts and ask the Treasurer to go through them with you to make sure you fully understand where the club has come from and where it is going. By looking at the club accounts you can spot any errors/investment mistakes that have long since been written off as losses (or may even still be on the books). Do remember, though, that all clubs will have errors of some kind, although usually minor.

Approach other members and ask if they are still happy with the club strategy; is there a ground swell for change. The classic disaster scenario would be the club changing its investment philosophy and strategy just after you join, and you not being happy with that new philosophy.

Does the accounting system easily allow you to join, e.g. do you have to buy in to match all other member's investments or is there a unit investment approach?

How to Buy into a Club

Now, you might think that if each existing member is worth a reasonably tidy sum, the total club worth may *look* prohibitively high for buying in; so how will you afford it? The club may have an accounting system that will permit new members to join from scratch with a modest buy-in or simply with standard monthly contributions.

Take, for example, a club that has ten members, each with a personal worth of £1,000. The club net worth is therefore £10,000.

If you want to buy into this club as a new member, you must start from scratch, purchase a fractional part or pay in a lump sum, the equivalent of each member's personal worth. There are three practical options:

Option A is to buy-in with a £1000 lump sum and match each member's stake. You are then on an equal financial footing with all members.

Option B is to buy in a fractional part of £1000, e.g. £200 that will equate to 20%. You then own 20% of a member's holding, which is 2% of the club's net worth.

Option C is simply to start making regular monthly contributions and build your stake over time.

Of course this will mean that your individual worth will be lagging behind all the others. However, there is nothing to stop you from boosting your investment by adding a lump sum as it becomes affordable should you have a windfall of some kind.

Summary

✔ Opportunities to join established clubs may be few.

✔ You can search for a club, but it can be difficult and may not meet with success - better to start one.

✔ Before joining any existing club, be sure their strategies are aligned with your own and assess the member types for compatibility.

✔ Check that the accounts are in order with a history of good or at least average club performance.

✔ You can start contributing once you are formally accepted into the club.

Chapter 6

Making Investment Selections

THIS IS, of course, the most exciting part, where the meetings liven up as members debate which shares should be bought and sold.

It is worth asking at the outset if any members have specific principles or moral values which would prevent them investing in certain companies such as those which produce tobacco products, armaments, genetically modified foodstuffs, etc. It's best to establish if anyone has these concerns and get them out into the open so that conflicts do not occur.

Let us take a brief look at shares to explain exactly what they are; this will help you understand later sections.

Shares - An Overview

What is the stock market? It is simply a central place where company shares are bought and sold by anyone, from big institutions such as pension funds, to ordinary investors.

A share is exactly as it suggests, a part ownership of that company. Your share holding will be a fraction of the total value of the company. This fraction will be dependent on the number of shares in issue.

Shares are in themselves a risk; their value could decrease. In general, though, if you can ride out any slumps, shares do outperform the returns on funds deposited at banks or government loan instruments in the long term.

Do not even contemplate investing in shares with money that is essential and on which you are dependant. It is only when you have sufficient emergency funds and your other financial matters are secure that you should consider buying them. You should realise that it is money that you may not be able to get back at short notice.

Investment Opportunities - Where to find them?

Ideas for investment opportunities can be gleaned from many sources. These may typically be broadsheet newspapers, magazine articles, private investor journals, the Internet, television, through work contacts and most importantly by your own observation of the world around you.

From newspapers, magazines and the Internet you will read first hand about companies in the news. A tried and tested approach is to look for stories on big companies with powerful brands and corporate images. Assess their performance by reading as much as you can about them. Is the news generally good? Try to decide if they are on the up and making the right kind of strategic decisions to enhance the company's performance and hence the share price. If you stock pick by pinpointing individual shares, and get it right, you are likely to get far better returns than if you held a tracker fund following any one of the major markets.

By keeping your eyes open and observing the world around you may notice a new craze the kids are getting into, for example - who manufactured it, what are the company's other interests, are they working on the next craze, what is their finance structure like, is there an investment opportunity there?

Investment decisions at Meetings

Ideally, you should have come up with your list of potential companies for investment before you arrive at the first meeting. Armed with your research you must then enter the arena of your club meeting prepared to do gladiatorial battle with your fellow researchers. Then the club will go through the formal route of making final investment decisions via a process of discussion and debate.

Each member should have his/her turn to present their information to ensure it is a truly democratic process. The group must then decide on which way to invest and how much to invest (remember your financial strategy). The usual practice is for decisions to be made on a majority basis, e.g. six from ten for example. Any less than the prescribed quota in favour and the decision has to be deferred.

Remember to closely monitor any stocks that did not make it as buys, but which were thought to exhibit some promise. These may be good buying opportunities at a later time.

Where to Get Information

Where are you going to find the information that you need to make informed investment selection? Information gathering should be as widespread and varied as possible and practicable for you. It is usual for clubs to utilise multiple sources of information for data collation. This is an ideal approach and is strongly recommended for which all members should be encouraged to participate.

Newspapers

Newspapers are the most popular source of information amongst Investment Clubs with ninety five percent of all those clubs surveyed saying that they use the business columns for up to date news of what is happening. Not only can you find company related news stories but all the facts and figures that you need to get started on your research e.g. daily share price, market capitalisation, P/E ratio, dividend yield, etc.

The Internet

The Internet provides instant access to a wealth of information on a host of companies and is used by more than 64% of Investment Clubs as their main source of information when selecting and monitoring shares. It has the advantage of near real time news updates and, of course, can be customised for your exact requirements. The best way to make use of the plethora of information is via one of the many dedicated financial sites that provide company news, accounts, past performance and share price data.

Most sites are free to access at a basic level. The data you'll have access to, however, will be 'delayed' by 15 to 20 minutes. This will satisfy the needs of the majority of Investment Clubs. Should you deem it necessary to have access to real-time data, then you will probably have to subscribe to their 'premium' services (for which you'll receive other additional services such as extra analytical tools).

Another useful feature of the Internet is the 'bulletin board'. In these discussion areas you can reap the benefit of other's knowledge and participate in topical debates. Beware, though, of 'rampers' who deliberately talk up (or down) the prospects of particular stocks, in which they have a holding, so as to manipulate the price.

Tip Sheets/Newsletters

These are often very detailed with broker forecasts and comprehensive chart analyses thrown in, but you have to pay for the privilege and it can be quite expensive. You have to decide whether the cost of subscribing can be repaid by astute investing resulting from the information gained.

When share trading is in large quantities, the market tends to be somewhat frenzied, rather like a shark feeding when it has a substantial appetite. It is at these times that 'Hot Tips' are the talk of the town and it is often very common to hear people discussing shares in the same way as discussing recent sports results.

These so called 'Hot Tips' are often related to Penny shares. Now think about this point carefully - if someone really had excellent information, (perhaps even insider) then would they make it available to all and sundry? Instead, the tip is likely to be an attempt at ramping the share (promoting it vigorously in order to increase buying volume and hence drive the price up.)

So, can you trust the information that is printed in tip sheets? Some are good, have good reputations and authors with solid financial backgrounds but others are little more than company brochures espousing their virtues. But always bear in mind you will not be the only person to receive the tip-sheet. If a quantity of sheet recipients buy-in early, you may find you will be forced to pay a premium if the price has already rocketed.

However given all these words of caution, it is actually possible to use these tips successfully if your timing is good, but treat them cautiously.

Company Reports and Accounts

This is a good place to look for details on prospective companies. If you want to know more about a particular company, what better place to start than by analysing their own information?

Companies are required by law to produce a report and a set of accounts each year. And, if a company issues new shares to the public, it must publish a prospectus, which provides information similar to, and often much more detailed than, that provided in an annual report and accounts. These documents give you a very good grounding in the company's activities as well as its current performance and prospects.

What should you look for in a company's reports and accounts? There are key areas of particular importance, they are:

- Past profitability
- How effectively new investment has generated further profits
- Where the company's capital comes from and how much it costs them
- How many shareholders have to share in the profits

It can be a complex area to sift through and you will need to build your understanding, but at first concentrate on the summary accounts, follow the notes scattered throughout the document and trace them to footnotes and compare the figures with those for other periods, (i.e. look for trends). You will soon see a picture of the company's financial status and prospects beginning to emerge.

Your Portfolio

A 'portfolio' is the term used for an owner's total holding of shares or other investments. There are a number of factors to consider when you begin to consider building your portfolio. For example, how many different shares will you buy and hold at any one time? Too few and you will not have sufficient sector diversity, and too many means that you may not be able to monitor them all efficiently. There are no hard and fast rules about portfolio size, but a general rule of thumb seems to suggest that between eight and twelve is a good number to aim for.

Equally important is the balance of your portfolio, i.e. your purchases should be from different market sectors, different risk categories and balanced in terms of the overall contribution to the portfolio; no single company should dominate. This chapter elaborates these points providing an insight into portfolio balance, what to look for in an investment, risk types and finally what does not constitute a suitable purchase for an Investment Club.

Ideally you will form a balanced portfolio, e.g. holdings in long term steady growth stocks, some in medium risk rated stocks and some in high risk. The higher risk element does stimulate interest, as it is generally more volatile; that is the price can make larger moves (both up and down) more frequently than blue chip stocks. Higher risk buys therefore require constant monitoring and hence vigilant members.

In the early stages of running a club, however, and certainly if you are new to shares, it will make more sense to avoid high-risk investment until you know what you are doing. Learn the game and gradually delve into the higher risk shares and potentially higher rewards when you, as a club, feel more comfortable doing so.

The following illustration shows what could be regarded as a typical club portfolio and one which includes more of a speculative element. This way of balancing a portfolio is often known as following the 'Pyramid Principle' and is intended to ensure that you do not end up with a top heavy portfolio.

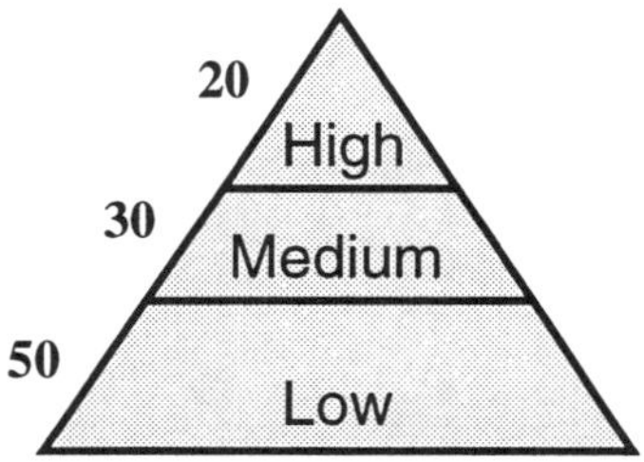

A typical portfolio

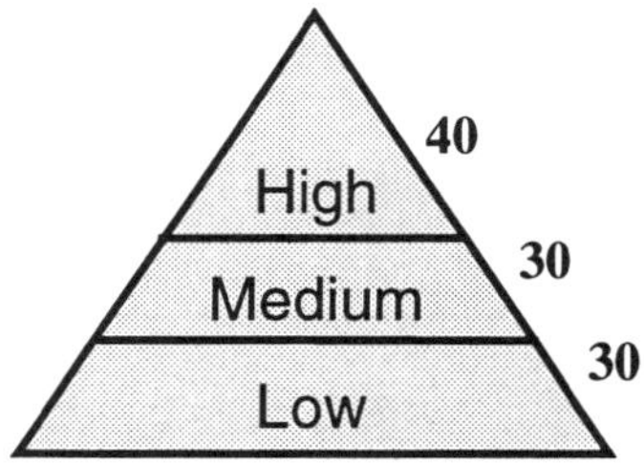

A more 'speculative' portfolio

It is also good practice to invest in companies in different market sectors as this will give a degree of protection against swings in certain sectors; as everyone saw when Internet and telecomms stocks plummeted after the so-called 'technology bubble' burst. This approach is regarded as having a 'diverse portfolio' e.g. one spread across a range of companies in the stock market. Remember that diversification helps spread both Risk and Opportunity.

What are you looking for in an investment?

Having found your little gem of a tip you must then research it and monitor it. What is the core business of the company and is there any peripheral business? What is its share price and how does it fluctuate from day to day and week to week? What volume of shares is typically traded each day? Does it pay a Dividend? If so how much? Is the company ever mentioned in the newspapers? If so, what is being written about them? Is it generally positive news or negative? What is the financial set-up and status of the company (Market Capitalisation)? How much do they spend and how much do they make? Who are the directors, what is their track record? Where is the company going and what is it trying to achieve? Are their targets realistic? These are questions you must be seeking answers to.

Growth Stocks (Low/Medium Risk)

Growth stocks are shares that will grow steadily in value over time, providing you with increased capital gains. Although growth stocks can encompass a range of stocks over a spread of indices, you should consider only the companies with a large market capitalisation. These stocks are typically in the top 250 companies listed on an exchange.

It is worth mentioning Blue Chip companies as an aside. These are considered to be sound investments at the low- to medium-risk end of equity dealings. It refers to the type of company that is long established with solid business credentials and that is unlikely to fail.

Of course this does not guarantee the share price from falling. Even Blue Chip companies can let you down, but over the long-term and on average they should show steady growth.

The basic necessity you are looking for is share growth over the medium- to long-term (increase in value of the share over time).

Earnings Per Share Growth.

Earnings Per Share (EPS) is defined as the total after-tax profit of a company divided by the number of shares in issue. A number of investment gurus point out that EPS should increase by at least 15% per annum every year. Occasional years of no growth can be tolerated but on the whole the trend over five years must be up.

Price to Earnings Ratio

The Price to Earnings Ratio (P/E Ratio) is defined as the current share price divided by the last known EPS. So, for example, if a company A earns 5p per share (EPS) and the current share price is 100p then the P/E ratio is 20. The higher the hopes for a stock the higher the P/E ratio associated with that stock.

If the calculation has used actual past earnings information then this is known as an historic P/E ratio. This historic P/E ratio is based on factual, published past earnings information. If the P/E calculation has used predicted earnings information then this is known as a prospective P/E ratio. The prospective P/E ratio is effectively giving you the market's opinion on the stock's future potential. Make sure you know which one you are dealing with.

This P/E ratio can be a useful tool in comparing companies, especially within the same sector. If you can identify stocks with a P/E ratio at less than the sector average, then this stock may have room for an increase in the share price.

High P/E ratios could mean that the price of the stock is too high. Investors are already aware of this stock and have pushed up the share price. This stock will have to perform exceptionally to meet expectations.

Low P/E ratios may reveal lack of investor confidence in a stock but could identify an undervalued share which could be an ideal investment opportunity. Do your research on these low P/E stocks - why are they low?

It is critical to compare the P/E ratio of a stock to the sector in question and the market as a whole. You have to be sure that the P/E ratio you are dealing with has not been affected by other external factors. Perhaps higher interest rates have knocked the stuffing out of the markets and P/E ratios are generally low. The tail end of an economic recession may yield higher than expected P/E ratios with the anticipation of recovery. During bull markets P/E ratios may typically be artificially high and during bears they may be low. Also keep in mind the kind of stock that can have high P/E ratios, like mining or oil companies, where the market is considering the assets ahead of earnings.

Dividend Yield

A dividend is a distribution from a company to a shareholder in the form of cash, shares, or other assets. The most common kind of dividend is a distribution of profits to shareholders.

Dividend yield is the dividend divided by the current share price, expressed as a percentage. It is useful for income investors who want to compare the yield of a particular share with yields from other shares and, perhaps, other types of investment.

A business with good profits potential will generally have a relatively high share price, which will tend to provide a low dividend yield. Conversely a company whose prospects are not well-rated will tend to have a low share price which can produce a high dividend yield. You can only assess whether a dividend yield is abnormally high or low by comparing with the company's yields in previous years. You should also take into account the yields available from other shares in the same sector and the market as a whole.

Risk Investments

Higher risk shares like Penny shares offer potentially higher rewards, but also carry a greater chance that you might lose money on them. Having decided your club's investment strategy and considered (and possibly even invested in) the lower- to medium-risk growth shares you could now be looking for a bit of a gamble. Buying into this market can be great fun since the risks are realised to the full. You may make your fortune with this type of stock but equally you could lose it all.

'Penny' shares are typically small companies with low market capitalisation and a low absolute share price. These companies can, on occasion, be a more profitable investment than larger companies simply because it is easier to expand from a smaller base than a larger one. The rapid rate of growth will then be reflected in the rapid rise of the shares' value. However it may be the case that these small companies are walking a financial tightrope, with greater reliance on bank finance in comparison to their larger counterparts. These have a higher chance of failure.

Share Price

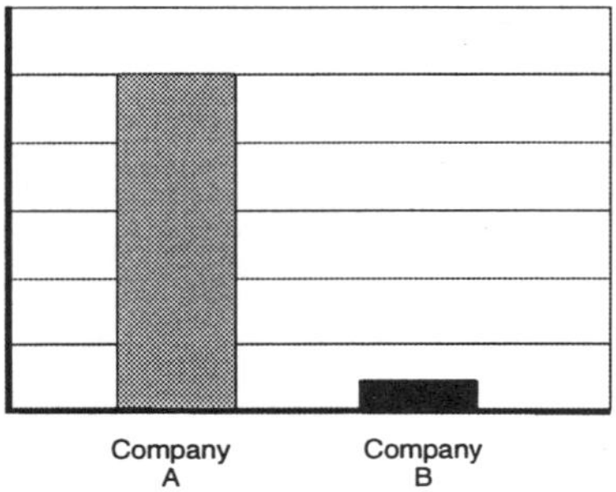

Shares in Issue

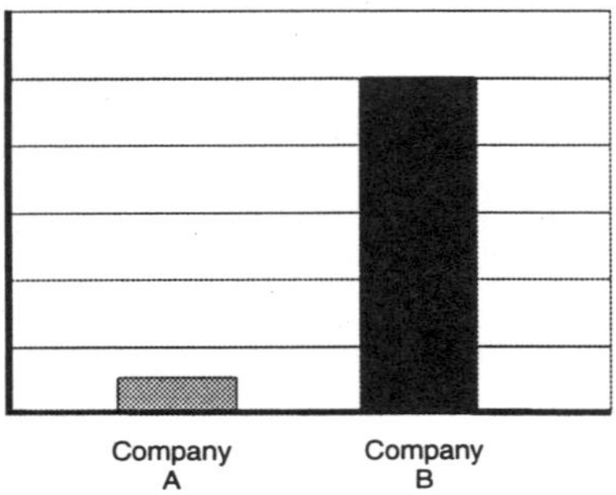

Market Capitalisation

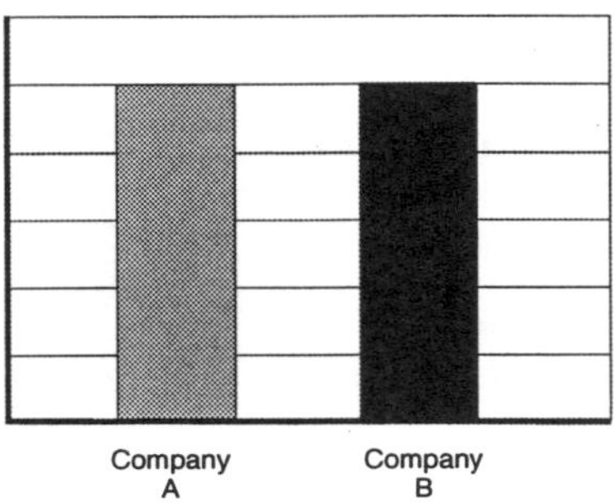

Do not assume that Penny shares are necessarily cheap just because you can buy many more shares in them over other higher priced shares for the same amount invested. The share price in effect tells you nothing on its own; you have to take the market capitalisation into account as well.

For example, if company A's share price is 10p and company B's is 1p you might assume, initially, that the 1p share may be cheaper than the 10p share. Further investigation may reveal that both companies have similar assets/debts/ earnings and similar market capitalisation of £100,000, but company A has

1,000,000 shares in issue and company B 10,000,000 shares. Thus the fact that company A is a Penny share and B isn't has little bearing on their 'worthiness'. The illustrations, above, may help you visualise the situation.

Another factor to consider when buying Penny shares is the bid-to-offer spread. When you buy you will pay the ask/offer price and when you sell you get the bid price; with Penny shares, the difference can be a large percentage of the absolute price. Then, when you throw in the dealing cost, the price of your Penny shares will have to increase dramatically just for you to break even.

For example share A's mid price is quoted as 7.5p. You buy at the offer price of 10p. The bid price is quoted as 5p. In essence, at the moment of purchase, you are now in loss territory. You've paid 10p share and now it's actually worth 5p per share to sell. This means you now have to make 100% return on the 5p bid price of the share just to break even (without considering the buy/sell charges). Although this is an extreme example the principle always stands. Do your sums for any prospective purchases while bearing these factors in mind.

One thing that is certain with Penny shares is volatility. The shares can appear dormant for many months, with little fluctuation of the share price, but a tip in the Sunday press by a respected financial journalist can see prices moving upwards as buyers follow investment advice and buy-in. Equally any negative news can affect the share price drastically. This news doesn't even have to have anything to do with that share directly. It could be affected by general market trends just as quickly as a direct profits warning. Generally you will not find Penny shares in sectors that are usually regarded as stable e.g. banking sector.

Only invest money in Penny shares that you can truly afford to lose. The fact of the matter is that some of your investments will fall in value. You are looking for the one winner, a gem of a share that is going to cover your other Penny share losses and give you something to smile about.

Income

Investing in equities for income is at the high-risk end of investment and should be considered only as part of a balanced income-generating portfolio.

When investing in equities for income you need to identify companies with high yields. These high yields can be the result of one of two reasons; the stockmarket is worried about future dividend growth prospects or there is an impending cut in the dividend. More soundly based companies will be valued by the market to return only a small yield.

Market decline can therefore provide an opportunity to buy high-yielding stock cheaply but you must ask for how long will those yields continue during an economic downturn?

For any projection of potential income from equities you must account for the tax you will pay on the income as well as the effect of inflation. Only then can you be certain that you are earning a real income or not. Do remember inflation will erode your investment capital. So, if over time inflation increases and your equity dividends are static in growth (or reducing) then you are making less money in real terms.

Investment Suggestions to Avoid

During your meetings many options for investment will be discussed. UK or US stocks and shares will probably be discussed most often, as will perhaps Mutual Funds such as Investment and Unit Trusts. There will come a time when club members bring up more alternative suggestions for discussion.

High Interest Deposit accounts… property for letting… lotteries… fine art… antiques… vintage wines... to be honest the list is almost endless. Under some circumstances investment in any from this list may be a good thing. Under the umbrella of a Investment Club the general rule should be to avoid them at all costs.

Investment in a high interest deposit account is a very low risk investment, constituting no excitement or learning process about the stock market at all. It is about as exciting as sucking a wet blanket. Yes, low risk investment is sometimes a good thing and often necessary if you want to achieve a balanced ('pyramid type') portfolio. However if you seriously consider lower risk investment like these, you might as well not bother with an Investment Club at all.

As for gambling (betting on horses, lotteries and the like), you will be throwing your money away. Sure, investing in stocks and shares is a risk, but it is a calculated risk - gambling on the other hand, is calculated madness. Again this isn't a lecture against gambling, just that it is not the right thing for an Investment Club. Losing money always conjures up negativity within a club and members can lose interest quickly when on a losing streak - you increase the chance of this negativity by gambling away your money.

If you are in a big money Investment Club then the topic of investing in property for letting may crop up. Think very carefully about this one. Research all the costs involved (solicitors, estate agents, management fees, your time, etc) and then weigh up whether it is worth it. Usually it is not. Property can be a great investment proposition for some individuals but, again, not for an Investment Club.

As for antiques, fine art, vintage wines, etc., you can guess where the thread is going based on previous comments... forget it. You may have seen programmes on television where fine pieces of art or antiques are valued at astronomical sums. The items you see are usually family heirlooms and to acquire them, other than through family, would entail paying a fair sum, unless you find a real bargain. This, of course, means that it may take a decent length of time, (quite possibly years) to achieve a higher valuation than you paid in the first instance.

One of the main reasons anyone would buy a painting or an object of art would be for its visual attractiveness. It has to look good and mean something to you. You have to really know your market to invest in something that would be attractive or mean something to someone else.

The bottom line is that in order to make you money you would have to sell it on at profit. But art is generally regarded as a longer term appreciating asset. You have to be very lucky (or know your subject matter very well) to sell on at profit quickly. And what do you do if you cannot sell the piece of art on? You have made an immediate loss and possibly lost all your investment (OK you still hold the object itself but that is not the point of your Investment Club - you are in it to make money). Remember art fashions change as often as the wind. What you buy today as a fashionable investment may very quickly fall out of fashion tomorrow. This, of course, means that your purchase will be difficult to sell.

Also you must consider the provenance of the object. Is it what you think it is? Does it come from where you think it does? Could it possibly be a fake? You have to know your subject matter very well indeed.

Finally, there is also the problem of where the object is to be kept once purchased. You are a club with several members - who is prepared to look after it? Think of the possible increased insurance costs. Will you have to buy secure storage, how much will that cost? If you are holding the piece long term it will need the correct treatment or may require restoration work. This all costs money and digs into any potential profit.

Investing in any of the previously mentioned areas can be profitable, usually in the longer term, but are really for the more experienced individual investor looking to broaden his/her portfolio. Under the Investment Club umbrella, stick to stocks and shares. This is the bread, butter and jam of an Investment Club.

Summary

- ✔ Use all sources of information to help the club.
- ✔ Consider where you want to invest and be aware of problems with currency fluctuations and overseas markets.
- ✔ The Internet is a particularly good vehicle for locating data and information on the majority of investment opportunities.
- ✔ Use tip-sheets/Newsletters if you can afford it.
- ✔ Consider your portfolio in terms of risk factors and market sectors.
- ✔ Assess your proposed purchase very carefully - weigh up all of the pro's and con's.
- ✔ Beware the high risk and bid/offer spread in Penny shares.
- ✔ Know what does NOT constitute a club investment proposition.

Chapter 7

Monitoring and Selling Your Investments

HAVING LOOKED at the various investments the club can enter into, it is time to look at a much-neglected aspect of investing - when to sell. Remember, a profit is only a profit, once you have sold your investment. In this chapter you will learn how to monitor your investments and under what conditions you should consider selling. The mechanism of stop-loss is explained, as is the need to set profit targets.

Monitoring Your Portfolio

There are many ways of monitoring your chosen investments, and the best one for your club will depend on the knowledge of your membership and on the amount of spare time they have to apply the techniques. Essentially you are faced with using technical analysis, which uses graphs and data to make predictions, or by keeping an eye on both macro and micro economic events.

Technical Methods

Techniques range from very simplistic pencil-and-paper methods to more complex computer-based software tools with clever analysis algorithms. Each has its own inherent advantages and disadvantages. The simplistic approach, (pen and paper recording) is not very dynamic, providing you with a series of snapshots that are soon outdated. This is really only suitable for long-term buys that do not change rapidly with time i.e. have little volatility. On line and computer-based monitoring can provide you with up-to-the-minute information and you have the added benefit of being able to apply complex calculation algorithms at the click of a mouse. It is very dynamic and enables you to monitor rapidly changing share values with ease.

As already implied, the frequency with which you monitor a share will very much depend upon its volatility. If an investment's price is changing rapidly in a short period, say under a week or even daily, then your monitoring frequency will need to be increased to match. Rapid daily fluctuation will require intra-day, perhaps even hourly monitoring. If it is a 'steady' type share, purchased for the medium term, then the share price will not change much during the course of a week or maybe a month and this should be monitored on a weekly basis.

You will need to decide into which categories your purchases fit in order to make a good estimate at the necessary monitoring frequency.

Traditional Methods

The old favourite amongst those who prefer pen and paper is the Share Purchase Record. This is simply a table used to record the price changes of all shares owned by the club on a weekly or daily basis. You can then easily visualise how the share price is performing over time without the aid of technology. Simply plot the data on an X/Y chart, where X is the bottom line of the graph

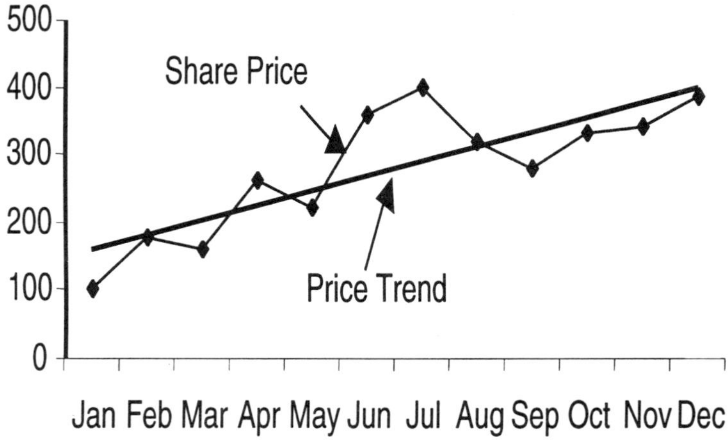

representing time and Y is the vertical axis and represents the Share Price. Simply mark a dot against price and the date for each recorded value. This will then indicate a trend or pattern of how the share is behaving.

The concept of pen and paper recording is preferred by many and has lots of benefits. It is always available, is easy to employ without a PC and provides an at-a-glance record. If you are technology orientated, then it will not be your thing, but if it's simplicity you want it will work for you.

Modern Methods

There are some excellent Internet sites that offer you the opportunity of 'free' portfolio monitoring. These usually work on delayed price information (usually by around 20 minutes). You will only need to register details and set-up a password. However, if you want real-time dealing figures and trade information then you will probably need to pay for it via a subscription (or it may be offered as a freebie by your stockbroker).

Many sites also offer powerful analysis tools with many enhanced features such as your portfolio's performance over a user-specified period.

You should also be aware that there are off-the-shelf software programs available to run on your home computer. These rely on data downloaded from the Internet, but leave you free to perform your own analysis whilst offline.

Director's Dealings

Director's dealings are regarded by some as a good way to judge a company's health. The thinking is that if the people who run the company are buying shares, then it must mean that they have confidence in the company and future performance. Conversely if they are off-loading holdings that would also show that they have a lack of confidence in future prospects and are looking to cash in.

Importantly when you look at director's dealings pay attention to the size of the deal. If it's small, the deal may well just be a personal fundraising or tax issue.

Management Changes

A company may have built a reputation based upon its leadership and there may be figureheads in the organisation who command respect within their operating sector. If they leave, defecting to pursue a better offer or retiring this can affect the share price quite dramatically. Sometimes entire management teams are head hunted by the opposition with quite disastrous effects if the raid is successful.

Fashion

Not in the literal sense as we know it but more in what sector is likely to come to the fore and become the next 'sexy sector' to invest in. These sectors may gain value and advance more rapidly than others, providing buying opportunities. These are investor fads, where preferences created overnight disappear with the same rapidity. The simple truth is that there is nothing you can do about these things other than to be aware that they will have an influence.

World Events

Global markets seem to rise and fall in sympathy and are influenced by world events such as oil shortages and military actions. Just take a look at the Dow or the Frankfurt Bourse and plot its performance against the London Stock Exchange. The similarities are quite remarkable.

The Economy in General

Inflation and interest rates are constantly on the move and can affect the price of individual stocks (particularly those with high borrowings) sectors and whole markets.

Currency Exchange Rates

These can have advantageous or adverse affects on a company's bottom line. If there is a high dependency on overseas trading then a change in current rates can be significant, as it will affect sales or purchases of either the company's saleable product or the commodities it needs to manufacture the product.

Taking Action

When to sell is the trickiest of all share-dealing decisions you will ever have to make. Running a stop-loss system will help as there is no argument and decisions are clear. However, there are other factors to consider when reviewing a share.

Stop Loss - Sell All

There is nothing complicated about the Stop Loss system. It is a simple, mechanical method ruling out emotion and following the most basic of investment rules, which is to run your profits and cut your losses.

Every time the club buys a new shareholding, you need to set a price at which you will sell, should it fall back in price. This price is known as the 'Stop Loss', as it stops you losing more money!

A good start is to set the Stop Loss price 20 percent below the buying price. Penny shares require a bigger margin, say 25 -50% due to increased volatility.

Never be tempted to change your Stop Loss once it is set. If the price falls to or beyond the Stop Loss, then sell. If your share rises, move the Stop Loss up behind it. If for example, you buy at 100 pence, you might set a Stop Loss of 80 pence. Move your Stop Loss up to 88 pence if the share price goes to 110 pence. If the price reaches 150 pence, the Stop Loss is simply 120 pence. If it should then fall from 150 pence to 120 then you will have 'banked' a profit of 20 pence per share.

Sometimes the system will fail you - you will sell, and the shares will rebound. On other occasions the price may plunge way below your Stop Loss before you can sell. However, the system is workable most of the time, and encourages regular monitoring of prices.

Overall, the Stop Loss allows you to choose how much you can afford to lose. It stops you convincing yourself to hang on for the recovery that might be just around the corner, which may never happen.

Always use the Stop Loss system, as it should be practised, with no emotion or other consideration. In a situation where the value of your stock is depreciating it is important that you preserve as much of your original investment as possible.

Profit Targets - Sell All

Just as you should implement a stop-loss system, you should set profit targets or trigger points. These will be pre-agreed values which, if attained, trigger a vote to sell the share. They are best set at a fixed percentage above the purchase price to achieve a desired cash sum clear of dealing costs. When your profit trigger has been reached you must instigate the vote, (a nominated individual responsible for monitoring the share may do this) and, if carried, sell.

Here's an example: Barry has been asked to monitor a share for which the club paid £1 per share. They purchased 500 shares in total and the club membership agreed a fair return, after dealing costs would be 40%.

The total outlay was £500 plus dealing costs of £25, (buy and sell) which is £525. To make the 40% cash return on this buy, the sale will need to realise £525 + £210 which equals £735. Therefore when the shares reach a value of £1.47 Barry has to notify the membership who then vote as to whether the holding should be sold or not.

Top Slicing - Sell Some

This is where you take some of the profit you have made in a stock, by selling a certain percentage. You may, for example, decide to sell 30% and leave 70% invested.

Note, though, that you can only sell a large chunk of your shareholding if it has seen suitable increases in value compared to the initial stake or it was a significant sum that you invested in the first place. It is no good selling 70% if you are left with next to nothing as a holding.

Taking the Stake Back - Pure Profit

When a share doubles in value from the figure that you paid for it, then sell half. For example, if you have 1000 shares originally invested at 100p per share, and the price rises to 200p per share, you should sell 500 shares; realising your original investment value and leaving the same amount to continue to grow. Then you are technically in a no lose situation. You've invested a sum of money, taken that sum of money back (ready for your next investment) and left your profit in the original investment. If that invested profit continues to do well - fantastic - but if it collapses then you've lost nothing but the profit - all your original investment money is safe. And if you also run the Stop Loss system, then you will also preserve the profit, albeit a reduced sum.

Other Sell Indicators

- **Sell if, on reflection, you think you may have made a mistake in buying the shares in the first place.** Perhaps it was a speculative hunch that did not work out or the company ran into problems. Maybe the company has evolved, their strategy has changed for the worse or they face stiff competition in their market sector and no longer appear to be a dominant force. Maybe they have divested too much or it is a different company now, capital intensive and low growth.

- **Sell if there is a better investment opportunity.** Always put your money where you believe it will bring you the best returns. This is especially so if a good new opportunity has arisen. The problem here is which shares do you sell? Usually, you should choose the worst performer - you need to cut out the deadwood and this is especially true in 'bear markets'. Do you still think the shares will do well in the future, have they done well recently and is value built into the price or are they likely to just 'tread water' from here on in?

Typically the worst performer may also be the one that you think is overvalued.

- **Sell if one or two companies are becoming dominant in your portfolio and it is unbalanced.** Better to spread the risk with multiple holdings. A rule of thumb is that no one company should contribute more than 33% of the total worth.

- **Sell if you need the money, for whatever reason.** If you can no longer afford to keep the money invested or can see a short-term need, say in under a year, then sell. Then you will not be left waiting for an opportunity to raise the necessary capital if you are unfortunate enough to meet with a correction, slide or crash in the markets.

There are other general questions that you should ask yourselves from time to time, such as how many shares are you holding at any one time and is it the right amount? What is a suitable quantity to hold and monitor? The key is to have enough shares to keep each member interested, but not so many that it's difficult to track them. Try not to allocate more than two shares per member for monitoring.

The Rule of Five

Regardless of how much research you do and how careful you think you are, investing is not an exact science, and you are most likely to encounter the 'rule of five'. It can serve as good guidance on what to expect from your stock selection.

The rule of five states that for every five shares you purchase, three will perform roughly in line with expectations. One will be a very poor performer and may fall flat losing you a considerable sum if you fail to act. If this is the case just accept the fact, dump it and accept the loss rather than paralyse your portfolio for the foreseeable future. The fifth however will be your star performer and will do far better than you would have imagined. These are the shares that stimulate interest and add excitement. They are the ones that you can boast to your friends about, e.g. how it made you a small fortune and what a genius you and your fellow members are.

Summary

- ✔ Review shareholdings regularly and set buy/sell targets.
- ✔ Employ a variety of monitoring methods - PC based alerts, WAP, manual records, etc.
- ✔ Monitor Director's dealings.
- ✔ Know what factors may influence a share price, i.e. world events, the economy, fashion, etc.
- ✔ Always employ the Stop Loss system.
- ✔ When considering a sale, decide how much of your holding to sell, some, all or none.
- ✔ Given an opportunity, always take the stake back or top-slice.

Chapter 8

Calculating the Club Net Worth

IT IS IMPORTANT for a club to know, (a) what the club is worth as a whole and (b) what member's personal stakes amount to. It is the treasurer's responsibility to report figures at each meeting, for payments made, received and the resulting balance. This chapter provides the detail with worked examples of how to make the relevant calculations.

Calculator 1

Members may want to leave the club and others may want to join, so it will be necessary to be able to quickly calculate a pay-off or buy-in value. Using a unit-based system makes this so much easier. Calculator 1 allows you to do just that; to work out unit values and hence individual worth at any time.

Unitising holdings in this fashion also allows members to leave the club totally, temporarily suspend their involvement or to increase their investment. Unitising also allows new members to join a club at any stage, as they do not need to match existing member's level of investment, they simply acquire less 'units' in the club. So they can buy in with a fixed number of units and add to these over time in the usual way.

The formula for Calculator 1 is:

$$A \div B = C$$

Where:

A is the existing value of all the club's assets. You arrive at this by adding the value of the share holdings to the cash in the bank and taking away any liabilities, such as bank charges, pending transactions, etc.

B is the total number of units bought by the members.

C is the *current* value of each unit.

Divide the value of the club's assets by the number of units issued to the members to give the current value of a unit.

Worked Example

In the following example, the club has 10 members, with each paying an initial lump sum of £50, followed by a monthly subscription of £20. All this money is then allocated to buy shares when there are sufficient funds.

Month 1

Everyone pays in £70 so the club has £700. The unit valuation system is based on £5 per unit so initially everyone has 14 units. At the first meeting the club decides there is not enough funds to buy shares yet, so it's carried forward to Month 2.

Month 2

All the members pay in £20 - a total of £200 for this month and a new member, Chris joins.

Chris pays his £50 joining fee and his £20 subscription, so he has 14 units and the original members have 18 units. The club has £970 in the bank, but decides not to purchase just yet, so this sum is carried forward. Of course Chris could pay in an extra £20 to give him the same number of units as the rest.

Month 3

Now there are 11 members in all who pay in their £20 subs for the month making a total of £1190 in club funds; (£970 forward plus £220 for month 3 subscriptions). The original members now have 22 units each and Chris has 18.

The club buys 200 shares in Acme Best Buy at £5 each at a total cost of £1030, taking into account dealing costs and stamp duty. This leaves £160 in the bank.

The shares rise by 125p to 625p, meaning the 200 shares are now worth £1250. Including the £160 in the bank, the total asset value of the club is therefore £1410. Since 238 units have been issued, you can divide 238 into £1410 to get £5.92 per unit.

This means that each £5 of an original member's subscription is now worth £5.92, the new unit value. So simply multiply each member's holding by this unit value to give each member's net value.

If someone new wants to joins at this point, they will need to buy-in at £5.92 per unit, no-matter how many units they want to purchase. Similarly, if someone wants to leave, they should be paid £5.92 for each unit they 'bought'.

Valuing and Auditing the Accounts

It is good practice to have a valuation day, that is one day in each month, which is agreed and is the designated date to calculate the club worth. Ideally this would be at or near the beginning of a month. If you implement this, then you will be keeping good track of your club's worth and hence its overall performance month by month.

It is essential to ensure that the accounts are audited at least annually. This is not necessarily to check the competence of the treasurer, but to ensure that mistakes are minimised. Errors that are found can be corrected by offsetting the figures accordingly.

Internal auditing also leads to familiarity with accounting techniques and the participation can improve member bonding. Alternatively someone could perform the audit from outside of the club. Perhaps they will do it as a favour, or be paid for their time. An external party can often be more rigorous and will generally be less afraid to report anomalies.

You should remember that although you will have an elected officer responsible for finance, it is each member's responsibility as an equal partner to ensure that the club's financial house is in order.

In preparation for Audit the treasurer should collate the following documents.

- All Bank account statements
- Any Brokerage statements - transaction details etc
- Any Profit/Loss statements from the Brokers
- Cheque Books and Paying in Books
- Any certificates that may be held by the club
- Financial reports issued since the last audit was carried out.

Once all the paperwork is in place it should be passed to the person(s) carrying out the audit who should document and report their findings in some detail. Other items that may be required are as follows:

- A transaction History for the audit period
- Member Details - Current members, past members and especially any detail on buy outs of departing members. Realistically just about everything relevant that comprises the accounts recent history. There is an obvious time of year to perform an audit, e.g. just after the end of a tax year. That way you will also have all the relevant taxation data if needed.

Alternative Accounting Schemes

There is an option to employ a simple percentage calculation, but often you will need to round up or down as the method will report two or three decimal places. It is a straightforward method

whereby you divide the total club worth by each member's monetary value or stake in the club.
Here is a very basic example, which indicates the problem.

Assume the club has ten members in total.

The total club worth is £1500 - From this total 10 members pay in £150 each

So each member with £150 owns ten percent [(£150 ÷ £1500) x 100 = 10%]

If the club net worth rises or falls, the individuals net worth will follow suit. So, should the club net worth increase by 10% to £1650, the individuals' stake is now valued at £165. Conversely if the club net worth falls by 10% to £1350 then each individual's stake is still 10%, which equates to £135

So far, so good, but things become a lot more complicated if someone joins the club later or wishes to pay in more money than other members; so now consider this situation.

There are still 10 members in the club but John decides he wants to pay in more, and the constitution permits it. So he adds another £100 to his personal stake. John has now paid in £250 and the other nine have paid in £150 each.

The total club worth is now £1600 and the percentages are calculated like this:

Johns share: (£250 ÷ £1600) x 100 = 15.625%

The rest of the members each own £150 each, so (£150 ÷ £1600) x 100 = 9.375% each

So as you see it can be done, but it is not as easy as a unit based scheme and could become quite complicated if members all contribute different amounts.

Summary

- ✔ Utilise a unit-based scheme to make the accounting straightforward.
- ✔ Dedicate a set day each month to calculate net worth.
- ✔ Do not forget to audit your financial records at least annually, ideally by someone external to the club.

Glossary

Agenda - A structured list of proposed proceedings for a club meeting.

Annualised rate of Return - Average return over a designated period of time (usually years) taking into account the effect of compounding.

Auditing - The process to verify that club records are accurate.

Balance Sheet - The part of a company's financial statement that depicts how a company is doing over the long term.

Bond - A debt security with a maturity of greater than one year from a corporation or Government body.

Bear - A investor with a pessimistic outlook of falling markets and share prices.

Bid Offer Spread - The difference between the bid price (at which the holder can sell shares) and the offer price (at which the holder can buy shares).

Blue Chip - A share in a bigger, safer, more prestigious company.

Broker - One who sells financial products of all sorts, not just shares. Has regulated authority to take customer orders on the sale of a security.

Bull - An optimistic investor, one who sees market increases ahead, good returns and a generally upward trend for the markets. The opposite from a 'bear'.

Buy-Ins - The amount you must pay to join a club.

Capital Gain - If you bought a share and sold it at a profit, then that is a capital gain.

Chairperson - The person who has formal control of a meeting and directs affairs.

Club Etiquette - The simple everyday courtesies that should be followed.

Constitution - The formally agreed and documented 'house rules' that the club will abide by.

Cost Basis - The purchase price you paid for your stock/share.

Dividend - A distribution paid from a company to a shareholder as cash, shares or other assets.

Dividend Yield - The dividend divided by the current share price, expressed as a percentage.

Earnings per Share - (EPS) Net Income divided by the current number of shares outstanding.

Ex-dividend - A share sold without the right to receive a dividend payment being made to those on the share register at a pre-announced date.

Exceptional Items - Items that feature in a Profit/Loss statement that are not expected to occur regularly.

Execution-only stockbrokers - Buy and sell shares on your behalf, generally have lower charges, but offer no advice. The shares are often held in nominee accounts.

Fixed asset - Something solid a company owns, e.g. land/property.

Goodwill - The difference between what a company pays for another company and the book value of that company.

Inaugural Meeting - The first official meeting of the Club.

Index - Benchmark against which to measure performance.

Institutional Investors - Institutions such as pension fund managers, unit trusts that are big players in the stock market and can often be major shareholders so have significant influence.

Liquidity - The easier it is to buy and sell an investment, the more liquid it is.

Market Capitalisation - The total market value of all the firm's outstanding shares, (that is those in issue). Calculated by multiplying a firm's share price by the number of shares in issue.

Member Types - The different characters and their personality traits.

Monitoring - Keeping a watchful eye on the value of your investments

Mutual Fund - An investment company that pools money from shareholders and invests in a variety of securities, such as stocks and bonds.

New Issue - the first time a company is floated on the stock market. Selling the company or part of it to outside investors can be a way to enable expansion plans. This is often known as an Initial Public Offering (IPO).

Nominee Account - An account in which execution-only stockbrokers hold shares belonging to clients so that buying and selling shares is quicker & easier.

Officers - Formal roles in the club that require election.

Penny share - A share which generally trades in multiples of a penny or less, are usually very volatile and subject to extreme price fluctuations on the flimsiest of rumours.

Price Earnings Ratio (P/E) - A measure of a share's price relative to its previous 12 months earnings per share. A higher P/E is generally indicative of sustainable growth, just what you want in a company.

Principal - The amount of money that is financed, borrowed, or invested.

Profit and Loss Statement - Explains how the balance sheet has changed over the year and gives a figure for the profits reported.

Profit Target - A trigger value at which you will sell a share.

Quorate - The minimum number of club members required to make a binding decision.

Non-Quorate - There are less members than specified to achieve a quorum.

Rights Issue - When a public company creates new shares. Existing shareholders can often be offered the right to purchase a number, usually at a discount to the market price.

Secretary - The elected official who deals with paperwork and other administrative duties.

Share - A security which represents part ownership of a company.

Start up Funds - The total amount paid into the club by members at its inception. This is usually larger than and in addition to the subscription.

Stamp Duty - A tax paid when shares are purchased

Stockbroker - The middleperson who invests your money, both buying and selling on your behalf earning commission on each transaction.

Subscriptions - The amount you pay into the club on a regular basis.

Ticker Symbol - The letters used to designate/identify a stock/share for trading purposes.

Total Return - Annual Return on an investment. This means the sum of an appreciation plus all dividends, interest and reinvested gains.

Treasurer - The elected official in the club who controls the books and reports figures and takes control of the accounts, etc.

Unit - The unit is a fractional part of the club's or an individual's net worth. It is used to simplify calculations.

Unit Trust - Your money invested with thousands of others in a pooled fund. Fund managers are responsible for achieving the fund's stated financial objectives.

Venues - Where you will hold your meetings.

Volatility - The degree by which a share price moves about. The more the price leaps about within a short time span, the more volatile it is.

Appendix 1

Inaugural Meeting

Apologies for absence - (from those who are unable to attend this meeting).

Take the contact details of all those present.

Discuss possibilities for the selection of a club name. (This can wait until the next meeting although you will not be able to set up accounts without it).

Election of a chairperson.

Election of a treasurer.

Election of a secretary.

Discussion and adoption of a constitution and club rules, how much money people are willing to contribute each month and whether there should be a membership fee? (Note the constitution may need amendments as the club progresses; be prepared for that).

Appointment of Stockbroker, (usually just the one) and types of shareholdings preferred.

Suggestions for a Bank or Building society to hold the account.

Discuss how subscriptions should be paid into the account and administered by the treasurer.

Discuss dates & venues for future meetings (say, for the next six months).

Set a deadline for when members must join the club.

Initial discussion on investment policy.

Any other business.

Date, time and venue of the next meeting.

Appendix 2

Constitution

The Club's aim - To carry out investments for its members with the aim of promoting financial gain and to act as a fun vehicle for learning about shares and other investment opportunities.

All members are committee members with officers elected annually at an AGM.

The size of the Membership is limited to 10 but may be reviewed annually at an AGM or EGM.

Named signatories to be principal officers, any two out of three.

Any additional or replacement members must be proposed, seconded and elected into the Club by the committee.

A quorum is to be 70% with at least two officers present.

An EGM is to be called by 60% of the membership.

Three months Notice of leaving the club should be given, monies due to the individual should be paid at the next quarterly review of accounts. This will be in the form of a buyout. Funding for any amount over £100 to be discussed further.

Voting rights regardless of personal worth are one member one vote with equal rights afforded.

Investments decisions will be made after due discussion in general meetings and the outcome will be based upon a majority decision of members in attendance.

All proposals must be included on an Agenda and a vote called for .

Proxy votes with respect to Club business will be permitted.

Payment dates from personal accounts into Club account to be the 16th of each month.

Frequency of meetings to be at least one per month on the first Tuesday of each month.

Stockbroker chosen as YourBank - Execution Only.

Monthly contribution is set at £30 reviewed at an AGM or EGM only, first payment to be either August 16th or Sept 16th dependant on when the account is setup.

Annual Membership fee to be £10 each cash to be paid to the treasurer.

* By Courtesy of Loss Amigo's Investment Club

Appendix 3

Agenda for an Ordinary Meeting

1. Apologies for Absence	Secretary
2. Financial Status of Club	Treasurer
3. General market condition/Topical Debate	All
4. Share Tips/investments	All
5. Decision Vote on Tips/investments	All
6. AOB	All
7. Date and Venue of next meeting (based on availability)	Secretary

Appendix 4

Reporting Obligations in the UK

The Financial Services Act 1986

This act covers Investment Clubs as well as other financial issues. You can be penalised for breaking its rules, so it's as well to be aware of the basic parts. If there is any doubt, always take legal advice.

It requires anyone carrying out investment business to be authorised unless his or her activities are excluded from the scope of the act. Members of Investment Clubs are exempt from the provisions of The Act providing they only act on their own or the club's behalf, and there is no payment involved.

Taxing Issues

Taxation is not a real issue for most Investment Club members. Any share dividends that the club receives will have been received after the deduction of basic rate tax and in order to qualify for Capital Gains Tax, (CGT), it would be necessary to make substantial profits. The latest CGT tax allowance details are available from the Inland Revenue.

To assist with tax declaration it would be advisable for the club treasurer to inform club members of their individual gain or loss at the end of each tax year. This is very easy to do, as most share -dealing accounts will send you an annual statement detailing transactions along with a profit/loss statement. That way each individual member can deal with his or her own tax issues.
So what do you need to do?

Notify the Inland Revenue of the existence of your club. The club treasurer should talk to someone in the tax office about the club and obtain the necessary forms to register. Exactly which steps you take will depend on the size and success of your club.

The Simplified Scheme

To qualify for this scheme, clubs must not have more than 20 members; subscriptions must be no higher than £1000 per member each year and net gains must not be more than £5,000 for the club in a year. Also the average investment per person based on cost price must not be more than £5000; and members must agree each year how to apportion Capital Gains Tax liability. In the UK you will need to fill in forms 185-1 and 185-2, (equivalents in the US) which you can get from the tax office or IRS.

The Standard form of agreement

After a while, perhaps a year or two, any successful Investment Club may exceed the conditions applicable to the simplified scheme as given above. With any luck this will be because net gains will have broken the £5000 barrier! If this is the case then the club will need to complete a standard form of agreement. The tax office will provide guidance to help complete the form. This is just the start, as each club member has to complete a tax return form 185.

It is usually a two-part form and should be completed for club members who have left during the year as well as for existing members.

Timing the Financial Markets

Charting your way to profits. Shows all levels of investors how to construct charts and graphs of price movements for bonds, shares and commodities. Then it explains, in easy-to-understand language, how to interpret the results and turn them into profit. With computers taking over so much of the trading activity on the world's stockmarkets (news programmes call it "automated trading"), charting is becoming a more and more powerful technique.

96 Pages *ISBN: 1-873668-47-3* *£6.95*

Investing in Traded Options

In jargon-free, easy-to-follow language, Investing in Traded Options takes all the mystery out of the options market. It successfully bridges the gap between the mundane experience of buying and selling shares and the exciting world of traded options.

You'll find simple examples, with accompanying diagrams, which will enable you to calculate and control the risks you are taking. By the end, you will have all the information you need to make informed decisions about the way you can use options trading to make extra profit or protect existing gains.

192 Pages (hardback) *ISBN: 1-873668-24-4* *£14.95*

Investing for the Long Term

This book is aimed at those savvy investors who are content to ride out short term fluctuations in the markets in order to realise bigger long term gains. Be it for school fees, a larger house or retirement, if you need money in more than 10 years time, this book is for you. Very comprehensive; covering everything from growth versus income to understanding company accounts, and from downturns, corrections & crashes to looking at the larger economic picture.

192 Pages (hardback) *ISBN: 1-873668-76-7* *£14.95*

Understand Shares in a Day

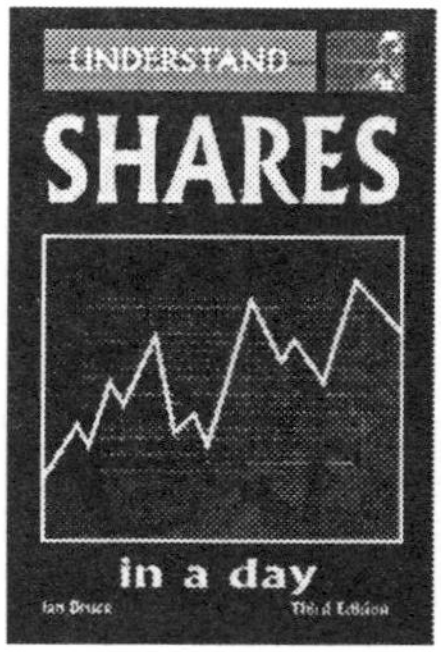

Shows how the share market really works. Inexperienced investors will learn: ❑ About different types of shares ... ❑ Why share prices fluctuate... ❑ How to read the financial pages ... ❑ How shares are bought and sold ... ❑ How risk can be spread with investment and unit trusts ... ❑ How to build a portfolio of shares ... ❑ The risks and rewards associated with Penny shares. Once this basic groundwork has been covered, the book explores more complex ideas which will appeal to both beginners and more experienced investors alike.

128 Pages ***ISBN: 1-873668-97-X*** ***£7.95***

Understand Bonds & Gilts in a Day

This handy title shows potential investors, and those with an interest in the bond markets, how to assess the potential risks and rewards, giving a simple to follow set of criteria on which to base investment decisions. Having shown the inexperienced investor how to go about buying bonds, it also teaches even the most arithmetically shy how to calculate the yield on a bond and plan an income based portfolio. The confusing terminology used in the bond market is clearly explained with working definitions of many terms and a comprehensive glossary.

128 Pages ***ISBN: 1-873668-72-4*** ***£6.95***

Understand Day Trading in a Day

Details how day trading works and how the private investor can become involved. It explains:

- ✔ What day trading is
- ✔ How it works
- ✔ Why day trading is becoming increasingly popular
- ✔ How to set yourself up as a day trader
- ✔ The mind-set necessary for day trading success

128 Pages ***ISBN: 1-873668-83-X*** ***£7.95***

Book Ordering

Please complete the form below or use a plain piece of paper and send it to the address given. You may also order online at www.takethat.co.uk.

Europe/Asia
TTL, PO Box 200, Harrogate, North Yorks HG1 2YR, England
(or fax to 01423-526035, or email: sales@takethat.co.uk).

USA/Canada
Trafalgar Square, PO Box 257, Howe Hill Road, North Pomfret, Vermont 05053 (or fax to 802-457-1913, call toll free 800-423-4525, or email: tsquare@sover.net)

Postage and handling charge:
UK - £1 for first book, and 50p for each additional book
USA - $5 for first book, and $2 for each additional book (all shipments by UPS, please provide street address).
Elsewhere - £3 for first book, and £1.50 for each additional book via surface post (for airmail and courier rates, please fax or email for a price quote)

Book	Qty	Price
	Postage	
	Total:	

☐ I enclose payment for £_______

☐ Please debit my Visa/Amex/Mastercard

No: ☐☐☐☐-☐☐☐☐-☐☐☐☐-☐☐☐☐

Expiry Date: ☐☐☐☐ Signature: ____________________

Name:Mr/Mrs/Miss: ____________________

Address: ____________________

____

____

Postcode/Zip: ____________________ Country: ____________________

invclub